WHO and WHAT IS GOD?

An exciting journey of discovery

"You need not that any man teach you:"
1 John 2:27

ALL YOU NEED IS TO DO IS TO
ASK FOR A LOT OF HELP FROM **HIM**

By
Brian H. Butler

WHO and WHAT IS GOD?

Copyright © 2019 Brian H. Butler

All rights reserved. No part of this book may be used or reproduced by any means, graphic, electronic, or mechanical, including photocopying, recording, taping, or by any information storage retrieval system, without the written permission of the publisher except in the case of brief quotations in critical articles or reviews.

This book consists mostly of prose expressions of the author's view and understanding of the Scriptures. It has few quotations from The King James Version of the Bible which is in the Public Domain, and is generally considered by most scholars to be overall the best translation despite its ancient English, and its many errors of translation which can easily be overcome and resolved by the careful, diligent student.

The publisher of this book may be contacted by email at:

bhb@ernestworkman.com

Because of the dynamic nature of the Internet, and web addresses or links contained in this book may have changed since publication and may no longer be valid.

The views expressed in this work are solely those of the author.

Perfect bound paperback book
ISBN: 978-0-9943391-7-1   paperback
ISBN: 978-0-9943391-8-8   eBook

Typeset by Brian H. Butler

Formatted by Angel Key Publications.com
Printed by Lightning Source

WHO and WHAT IS GOD?

WHO and WHAT IS GOD?

RELIGION	THEOLOGY
v	v
GOD — GOD'S WORD — The Holy Bible	**GOD** — GOD'S WORD — The Holy Bible
v	v
FILTER 1 — The Human Mind — The carnal mind is enmity against God, for it is not subject to the law of God, neither indeed can be — Romans 8:7	THE PURPOSE OF LIFE IS: To learn about God from the study of His Word & to strive to be like Him. Ask for, and receive it, **GOD'S HOLY SPIRIT FLOWS INTO YOUR MIND** The 'Light' comes on. New Understanding floods your mind & heart.
v	v
FILTER 2 — Truth mixed with error — Partial truths — False Doctrines - Idolatry — Human ideas & reasonings	**NO FILTERS** PURE TRUTH DIRECT FROM GOD TO YOU
v	v
FILTER 3 — Church organisations — Priests, Ministers — Desire to control followers	**YOU** — YOUR MIND — Your Human Spirit Enlightened by the flow of God's Holy Spirit, filled with the truth — The eyes of your understanding being enlightened; that you may know what is the hope of His calling, and what the Riches of the Glory of His inheritance in the saints. And what is the exceeding greatness of His Power to us-ward who believe, according to the working of His Mighty Power. Ephesians 1:18-19
v	
YOU — YOUR MIND — Your Human Spirit — Deceived into believing truth mixed with error — Having the understanding darkened being alienated from the life of God through the ignorance that is in them, because of the blindness of their heart — Ephesians 4:18	

TABLE OF CONTENTS

Bible Preface 1
How this book came to be written 1
Acknowledgments 5
Introduction 7
WHO and WHAT IS GOD? 9

CHAPTER 1
WHO and WHAT IS GOD? 11
The manual for human life 13
So how can we learn about WHO and WHAT GOD IS? 15
Before the 'Beginning' of all we know 16
God is a Being 16
God is Pure Love – Loving concern for Everything 17
God is Alive – The Life giver - The Mystery source
of all life 17
What does God look like? 17
God is All and in All. Some aspects of God's Beingness 18
Where did God the Father live before the foundation
of the World? 18

CHAPTER 2
God Created His Son – the Word 19
God is Timeless – and humans are bound to think in time 19
The planning phase of God and His Son 19

The formation & Development of 'The Plan of God' 19
The incredible complexity of God's plan 20
All this complexity without a Designer? 23

CHAPTER 3
THEN GOD THE WORD BEGAN TO CREATE ALL THINGS 25

First, the Word created Invisible Spirit Beings, Lucifer, & God's Sons 25

God Creates Spiritual Good and Evil 26

God's Secret Creative Powers were then used by the Word to form all things visible 27

The Three 'Heavens' of the Bible 28

The Energy of and within matter 29

Mathematics is a Power of God 29

New Geometry reveals another aspect of God's Powers 30

How much energy did it take to create the Universe? 31

The Cosmos - the universe as a system with an order and pattern 32

Our Solar System is different and very special 34

The Earth was formed to be inhabited. 35

The design of our Solar System and the Earth 36

God Created Time for us to experience a lifetime 36

Chapter 4
THEN GOD REFORMED THE EARTH TO MAKE IT HABITABLE FOR HIS CHILDREN 37

God the Word reformed the Earth to be inhabited in six days 38

Day One. God created light. He is Light 38
Day Two. God divided the waters and made
the 'firmament' the land 40
Day Three. God Created grass, herbs, trees 42
Day four. God created 'lights', day and night, seasons,
days and years 43
Day five. God made all the creatures that have life 44
Day Six. Then the Word Created the Human Man
and the Woman 44
How are human beings exercising 'dominion'
over God's Creation? 46
The 'Mind' of Christ, Yah-Shua, gives us our
example of 'dominion' 48
Most of humanity has lost sight of and respect for
the God of Creation 48
Our 'Life-Force' is in the blood 49
Day Seven. God finished the heavens and earth and
rested from His work 50
God planted a garden in Eden 51
Capillary attraction, a Power of God defies gravity 51
Adam the gardener 52
God Creates Eve 53
The knowledge of Good and Evil 55
The Biggest Lie – you shall not die 56
So, Adam and Eve knew the difference between
Good and Evil 58
The Truth about Life and Death 58
Death – when you die you are dead 58

All humans have a human spirit 59
What happens to the human spirit when we die? 60
What about the resurrection we are promised? 60
The 'Fall of Adam' was part of God's Plan 61
The Flood of Noah did happen 62
The 'birth' of universal rebellion against God 63
Christ became the only human Begotten Son of the Father 66
The Word, the origin and true nature of who
Christ, Yah-Shua the man was 67
God is now working through the second 'Adam' 69
Where do God and His Son Live now in this age? 69

CHAPTER 5
IS GOD REALLY WORKING THROUGH 1000's OF DENOMENATIONS AND .ORGS? 71
Do those who are deceived know it? 72
Here is a reality check for church attendees: 72
Beware of false Ministers, religions, churches 75
Ten Essential Keys to better understanding of the Bible 77
So, who is God dealing with individually and
personally now? 78
Who is God working with specifically in this age? 79
God is calling individuals at this time in history 79
God knows each of the 'called' intimately, in every detail 81
God gives us strength and protection 81
God works with his 'ecclesia' His group - individually 81

The Christianity of 'Churchianity' has lost its way
because of 'Attitude' 83

Repentance means to change one's mind and behaviour 87

We need to control our own human nature, not other people. . 88

The human desire to control others 88

The spiritual armour of God protects us 90

CHAPTER 6

THE NATURE AND HEART OF HUMAN BEINGS 97

The heart 'attitude' in the Bible 97

Eternal life is a free gift for all, so what are
Christian works? 98

The Parable of the Talents or pounds 99

The Parable of the Talents and rewards 99

What does it mean to work out our own 'salvation'? 101

Work on living and acting out the 'fruits of the Spirit' 101

We need to develop the Mind of Christ. 104

What happens when Christ returns? 104

What happens in the 1000 year Millennium? 105

CHAPTER 7

THE DEVELOPMENT OF TRUE SPIRITUALITY 107

People do not learn from miracles 110

The Glorious future of Human Beings 112

Satan has deceived the whole world – why does
God allow it? 112

Humanity is wrecking our Planet 113

Wars 114

The 'Great Tribulation' 114

Our Salvation - planned before the world began 117

Who are the 'Called'? 117

The Joys of the 'Called', their freedom in Christ 119

Our Glorious Hope of the resurrection and Eternal Life 120

People who are alive or dead in Christ will be
changed at Christ's return 123

The Revelation of the Future, the coming of the
New Heaven and Earth 124

Postscript 125

WHO and WHAT IS GOD?

Bible PREFACE

How this book came to be written

As a child, my parents used to take me to church. When I was about twelve, I was asked to give the Bible reading which happened to be 1 Corinthians 13, known as the 'Love' chapter. I memorised it, and somehow, its content and the occasion remained with me. Although attending for many years, my whole experience could be summed up by saying, I never really understood anything. The odd parable, or the story of Jonah, but otherwise, nothing.

Once I left home at eighteen when I was called up to do my National Service in the R.A.F., I did not attend any services at all. At twenty-two, I once went to a local church, but was so unimpressed, I never went again. I had always believed in God, and thought of Him as Creator, but I really was not interested at all in any religion. Frankly, even then, I thought, like so many do, that religious activities seemed to be at the root of many of the world's problems and wars.

Then I got the 'flu. Confined to bed, I started to browse some old copies of the Reader's Digest. Some advertisements took my eye. One said in bold lettering, 'Does God Exist?. Another offered 'Proof of the Bible'. There was no mention of a church, just the offer of some leaflets. I sent off for them.

I was taken by the style of the pamphlets, and that the writer clearly believed that the Bible was actually, really, the Word of God. Something went on in my mind, and I was very keen to learn more.

After a year or so of studying the written material and the Bible, I came to realise that there was an organisation behind it all, a church. I wrote off to them, and to cut a long story short, when I was twenty-five, I was invited to attend.

At twenty-nine, in 1964, I applied to go to the college which was run by the church, and was accepted for the four year, full time course, to major in Theology and obtain a Bachelor of Arts degree.

During my four years in college, I was privileged to take several courses with Dr. Ernest L. Martin, the Dean of the Faculty. His lectures were always riveting, and the most enjoyable as he made the history, geography, and the chronology of the Bible 'come alive' as I had never experienced in my life before.

After graduation in 1968, I was offered the opportunity to work for the College, and I gladly accepted a position in the data processing department, which was to stand me in good stead as time went on.

I also spent time with Dr. Martin between 1971 and 1974 after I was appointed a member of the Faculty of Ambassador College, Bricket Wood, U.K.

In 1975, my work with that church came to an end. Two years previously, in 1973, I had met and spent time with an American Chiropractor, Dr. John Blossom, who introduced me to a new concept in chiropractic known as Applied Kinesiology (A.K.) developed by Dr. George Goodheart. For the next twenty-five years I pioneered A.K. in Britain and Europe, ran a clinic of natural health care, and taught thousands the A.K. principles of self-help health care.

WHO and WHAT IS GOD?

In 2000, I retired after those years working in natural health care, helping the sick to work on their health and well-being, I once again turned to the study of Theology. The word Theology comes from two Greek words, Theo meaning God, and Logos meaning Word, hence Theology is the study of God's Word, the Holy Bible.

In 2013 I began an intense and in-depth study of over two hundred tapes recorded, and articles written by Dr. Martin on the fruits of his many years of Biblical research, kindly sent to me by Ken Nagele.

Working with Dr. Martin's material for 40-50 hours a week, using the essential 'keys' to understanding the Bible that he suggested the earnest Bible student employed, I learned more in the next three years than I had in over sixty years of my own personal previous study of the Holy Bible in my own strength. Since 2013 I have written well over a thousand pages of notes on Dr. Martin's Biblical doctrinal research. In my opinion these books contain the most important details of the fundamental basis of Christianity.

Excited at what I was learning about HOW to study the Bible with God's help, I wanted to share my new knowledge and approach with others. So, in 2015 I wrote 'Why ARE We Here?' a 382 page book which gave proof of the Authority and accuracy of the Bible, and the essential 'Keys' to a proper approach to the study of the Scriptures. This is available retail as printed paperback or an ebook from Amazon.com.

In 2016, I embarked my next book, 'The Biggest Lie and The Greatest Truth' 254pp. It addresses the lies of the 'Immortality of the soul', 'Churchianity, and the 'Theory of Evolution'. More importantly, it gives the 'Keys' on HOW to study, and grow in Grace and Knowledge, and a glimpse of the glorious future we have as Children of God.

WHO and WHAT IS GOD?

The next book, written in 2017 was, 'Discover more about God for yourself' 274pp., came about as a result of my last five years of an ever closer relationship with my Creator and His Son, and my intense personal study of God's Word.

This book you have in your hands 'WHO and WHAT IS GOD?, 126pp, was written in 2019, and updated in 2023.

In 2022, I wrote a more comprehensive book WHO and WHAT GOD IS – The Evidence and Proofs' of 400pp. It includes a list of many of God the Father's incredible Powers of Creation, of the Universe, our Solar System, the Earth, Life Force, the awesome complexity of DNA the key to all life, its fauna and flora, 'Photosynthesis', the energy produced from sunlight, glucose and water. 'Capillary Attraction' that allows fluids to flow sideways and upwards against gravity without which Godly Power nothing could grow; A possible explanation of the "Dinosaur Era", the absolute proofs that the Bible is the infallible Word of God, and an in-depth approach to Bible study.

My growing realisation of the Awesome Nature of God and His many Phenomenal Powers has changed my whole view of this human life and the Future we are Promised. As I have said before, previously I saw Theology in 'black and white and mono sound'. Now my appreciation of God the Father and His Son sees everything in 'glorious brilliant technicolour, and awesome stereo surround sound'.

ACKNOWLEDGEMENTS

In all my seventy-eight years I had often been exhorted to study the Bible, but I had *never* been taught *how* properly or systematically to study it. Dr. Ernest L. Martin, my colleague and mentor, showed me HOW to study. The first essential tool is always to begin by asking for God's help for inspiration and understanding. The wonderful Bible study 'tools' I learned from Dr. Martin and his tapes, also form the basis of my books on Theology, the study of the Bible.

*A note from the author: "I have absolutely no doubt in my mind that in this age, Dr. Martin was a (if not **the**) most remarkable teacher filled with the Holy Spirit, and that his insights and research were guided directly by God. I have found his work more inspiring than the work of any other man in my now eighty-three years.* **But please be very clear, in no way am I 'following a man',** *but merely using his tools. I am following Christ's Word, studying* **the Bible** *for myself,* **with God's help***".*

Dr. Martin said we never really needed him, but I feel God used him to help me to grow in grace and knowledge by leaps and bounds using the 'tools of the trade' he recommended; compared to sixty years of a lifetime of personal study in my own strength without them. I truly hope that the same may become true for those who read and study this book.

I want to express my deep gratitude and thanks to my daughter Claire for her many hours of diligent work in both proofreading and making my books. more readable.

INTRODUCTION

The purpose and goals of this book, 'WHO and WHAT IS GOD?' is to provide a resource to anyone whose 'eyes and ears' are being opened by our Father, the Almighty God.

God the Father, by means of the flow of His Power, Holy Spirit, will inspire their minds, to see the clear evidence of deception that the risen Christ, Yahweh-Shua, warned about in Revelation, the last Book of the Bible that God the Father wrote for our instruction.

*Revelation 12:9 And **the** great dragon was cast out, that old serpent, called **the** Devil, and Satan, which deceives **the whole world**: he was cast out into **the** earth, and his angels were cast out with him.*

When God and Christ say that Satan has deceived the whole world, They mean just that.

That includes **all** organisations of human beings. The Governments, the Philosophers, Scientists, the Religions, **all** are involved in the greatest deception possible.

In the realm of religions for instance, there are over thirty thousand separate denominations of what is known as 'Christianity'. They all work from the same Book, yet each one claims that their version of the truth, what they believe, teach and practice from their understanding of the Bible, is the correct one. They cannot all be right!

There can only be one version of the Truth. The Holy Bible that God the Father wrote through His Son is that Truth.

The original manuscripts, that were dictated to men who were inspired directly by The Word who became Christ, are the source of the Holy Bible we have today. Those manuscripts were perfect, exactly as God intended them to be. Since God created everything we know of, He is certainly able to cause men to produce the perfect Book He wants His children to use as their instruction manual for human life.

However, **all** human translations contain errors, made either by translators, or by organisations which have altered the Bible to suit their own agendas.

The earnest student of the Bible need not be concerned too much about the aberrations, as it is perfectly possible, when relying on God's help, to find a way past those errors, and be assured that what they are learning is indeed the Truth.

WHO AND WHAT IS GOD?

By Brian H. Butler

"You need not that any man teach you"
1 John 2:27

Author's note: This book is not about religion. It is about Theology, the study of God's Word. The Holy Bible is the only source of inspired Truths about God and His purpose for us.

WHO and WHAT IS GOD?

INTRODUCTION

CHAPTER 1

Who and What is God?

How can we know anything about a God? Simple really. One way is to observe and wonder at the evidence of His Incredible Mind at work all around us in this world.

The wonderful mystery His "Life-Force" itself, of the fauna, flora, and indeed in the construction and workings of the wonderful bodies we inhabit and how they function. Not to mention the orderly Sun, motions of the Moon, the Planets, Stars and the apparently unlimited vastness of the Universe.

Some say that everything in the Universe came from nothing and it all just formed itself one day with a 'big bang'. But can that truly be the explanation for everything? 'Everything came from nothing' has to be a false idea or belief.

Some 'theoretical physicists' (all theories are guesses, not facts) now suggest that everything came from nothing? Some magicians would have us think so with their illusions. But in our human experience, nothing comes from nothing. Everything starts in someone's **mind** with a thought, an idea. The idea becomes a concept, a design of 'something'. The materials for making the 'something' are planned and assembled. The 'something' is then made. So how could the incredibly vast universe and the millions of species on our Earth just 'happen' from nothing? No thought, no idea, no plan? On the other hand, many who subscribe to the 'theory' of evolution give credit for everything to 'Mother Nature' who or whatever that is; or in the case of one brilliant naturalist who enjoys a worldwide reputation, appears to give the credit to each species for being able to develop itself. This concept is sacrilege, stealing the credit for God's Creation and giving the credit to a 'Mother' who does not exist.

Some who support this theory propose that simple 'life' began in the sea. The suggested evolutionary process describes how 'simple proteins' assembled themselves into a form of 'life'. To start with, there is no such thing as a 'simple protein'. Science tells us that 'Simple proteins' are made up simply (?) of chains of amino acids held together by peptide bonds and folded or twisted in a specific way. So chains of amino acids joined themselves together? They do not do that now in a Petri dish in any lab. Are amino acids simple? The term amino acid is short for α-amino [alpha-amino] carboxylic acid. Each molecule contains a central carbon (C) atom, called the **α-carbon**, to which both an amino and a carboxyl group are attached. The remaining two bonds of the **α-carbon atom** are generally satisfied by a hydrogen (H) atom and the R group which is a side chain.

These very complicated amino-acid proteins then assembled themselves into a form that could move around, feed itself, excrete waste products, and reproduce itself? That is a lot to ask of a few chemicals floating around in the sea. They do not do that nowadays in a laboratory Petri dish either. Need we say any more?

It is even harder to understand how 'primitive' forms of life over millions of years gradually evolved the features they needed to survive without which they would have quickly become extinct. Yet many very intelligent, well educated people 'believe' in this proposition.

'Evolution' makes the truth of God's Creation into a lie, and in a sense the whole notion worships the creation instead of the Creator. Evolutionists exchange the glory and Power of the incorruptible God who made all things into the image and substance of physical humans, birds, four-footed beasts, creeping things and gives **them** the credit for their own design and development.

Nothing in our experience on Earth comes from nothing and makes itself. No rational thinking mind would suggest that. It just cannot be so. Magicians would have us think so with 'rabbits out of hats' and their clever illusions, but that is exactly what their 'magic' is, an illusion is a deceptive appearance or impression.

So, if everything could not have come from nothing, then somehow someone made it out of something. For ease, that 'Someone' we can call 'God', and He must have made it all out of 'Something'. He did. He made it Out of His Own Spirit Matter. Once the notion and existence of a 'Designer' is accepted, human beings can begin to appreciate and to be in awe of every complex wonder with which we are surrounded on Earth.

THE MANUAL FOR HUMAN LIFE

But how can we even begin to learn more about Who and What God is? God actually wrote a 'manual' that tells us all we need to know about everything in this life that we **cannot** find out for ourselves. The Creator God wrote that all time 'best-seller called the Bible. More Bibles have been printed than any other book ever published, by far. It is the only Book that explains in detail how the Earth and the Universe were Created, by the Creator.

God dictated to men, His servants, each of the books the Bible contains word for word which were to be painstakingly spelled out on the original texts exactly as He, God, wanted them to be written. Each page was then checked by specialist professional 'counters' who counted every letter of every page, and if just one letter was missing or incorrect, the page was destroyed. God wanted His book exactly the way He planned it to be and the original manuscripts are exactly that.

Men have made hundreds of different translations and they all contain errors, because each one includes human fallible ideas about God. But that fact does not need overly to concern anyone who really wants to learn the 'truth'. God can make sure that a diligent student will learn what He wants them to know at any given time in their lives.

Many say that the Bible is impossible to understand. They insist it is full of unbelievable stories, and contains many contradictions. As long as anyone thinks that way they will **never** even begin to understand it. Interesting, many who express these opinions have never actually read the Book.

Strange to relate, it is also a fact that the Bible was not written with the intention for it to be read and understood like any other book. The Holy Bible is not just another book, it is the 'Book of Truth' written by the Creator God, which contains the truths we need to know, and are here to learn in order to make a physical and spiritual success of this life. It is the most complex Book in the world, written over centuries by many different people, but it all fits accurately together faultlessly like one huge million piece jigsaw puzzle.

So, if we truly want to learn about God, we have to read the Book He wrote very carefully, **and <u>with His help</u>**. Without that 'help', the Bible appears to make no sense to the human mind, and is even inexplicable. So much of the Book appears to be nonsense to the unbelieving reader. It is said that 'seeing is believing' although in spiritual matters, 'believing IS seeing'. So with God's help and the right attitude we can begin to 'see' and to learn from the Bible a lot more about Him, and how to live this life.

WHO and WHAT IS GOD?

So how can we learn about Who and What God is?
His Book tells us that God is made of Spirit Matter and Spirit Essence which is invisible and indestructible, as are all His many Powers which extend everywhere, and are Omnipresent. God is the Origin of all Creation.

The Powers of God are still a mystery, and always will be. Atomic Energy, Life-Force, Gravity, Centrifugal Force, Magnetism and Electricity, the Electromagnetic Spectrum including Sound, Light and Radiation, and Capillary Attraction, are some of the Invisible Omnipotent Powers of God's Spirit which is why they will never be completely understood by ordinary carnal fleshly humans beings.

But that which we can learn about God will be made plain to us if only we look in the right place, firstly at our surroundings. Because God has shown us powerful evidence of His Invisible Power and Design in the tangible forms of all physical matter that we can touch, feel, and examine.

So the invisible things of God are clearly visible to us when we look at and study the creation of the world and the universe. Humans can begin to understand God by the things that He has made, and even learn about His Eternal Power and Godhead. So frankly, we are without excuse.

All Energy comes from God. 'Quantum physics' has enabled scientists to formulate many notions of how electromagnetic force operates within the atom, but they still cannot explain its Source. When 'science' is all boiled down, scientists think that all energy we experience on Earth is believed to come from the Sun's energy. Where the Sun's energy comes from nobody knows if they deny God.

In a sense, when scientists investigate what 'is' with ever more powerful instruments like the electron microscope and the Hubble and James Webb telescopes, and discover the existence of more and more amazing things, whether they appreciate it or not, since everything that 'is' and exists was made by God, they are actually learning more about God.

Before the 'Beginning' of all we know.

Before the 'beginning' of anything, God was. Before any 'beginning' we are aware of, and as far as we know, there was only God. There is only One God. God was, is and always will be. God is timeless, and is the 'Beginning' and the 'End' of everything.

God created 'time' for each of His human family to experience the lifelong process of being alive and conscious, and to enable them to learn about 'good' and 'evil'.

Some top brains in the world are wrestling with attempting to understand what exactly 'time' is. They will never work it out, it is one of God's secrets. Nobody can explain in detail the Nature of any of God's Powers. That is because they are the Secret Spiritual Powers of God, and humans will never fathom them no matter how hard they try.

A well-known phrase was composed by William Cowper written in 1773:

> God moves in a mysterious way
> His wonders to perform;
> He plants His footsteps in the sea,
> and rides upon the storm.

GOD IS A BEING –

God is Energy, He is All Powerful, All Energy and Power comes from Him.

Be-ing is the present continuous of the verb 'to be'. God always 'Was', 'Is', and always 'Will Be'. God is Past, Present, and Future, the simplest English word that expresses this is Eternal.

So, the word 'Be-ing' means 'to be' or to 'be existing' continuously, and in God's case without beginning or end. As long as they are alive, humans and all that has 'life' that has 'breath' on Earth, are 'be-ings'.

GOD IS PURE LOVE – Loving concern for Everything

God is Love. God is entirely Love. Everything He does is motivated by Love, a Loving concern for His entire Creation. Even in everything that is the opposite of Love in this present evil world, God's Love is in all. Without Evil, we humans could never begin to understand Love.

God's Love is vastly different and not to be compared with Human Love, which is only a shadow, a very limited dim reflection of God's Love for all His Creation.

God is also total Wisdom – Sophia, the female side of God is His Wisdom. God is innately 'male' and 'female' so He made His children male and female in His image.

God is ALIVE – The Life giver - The Mystery source of all life

God is Alive, He has Innate Life-Force, and has infinite Power to give 'life'. Life can only come from Life. God is 'Alive' and 'Conscious' and always has been, and always will be. God gives life, and takes it away. When He takes 'Life' away, it cannot be restored by humans.

God is the Source of all Life and Consciousness that exists in its myriad forms on Earth. Like all God's Powers, the 'Life-Force' is a mystery no human can completely understand. When 'Life' is present in any type of organism, that form is 'alive'. When 'Life-Force' is absent, that organism is 'dead', and cannot be restored to 'Life' except by the 'Life-Giver', God.

What does God look like?

God is Invisible to human beings. However, God's Spirit Matter has form and shape, and occupies space. God looks like a human being in shape, and has a head, eyes and ears, a body, and arms and legs. His eyes constantly run to and fro over the Earth watching over us. He sits, walks, feels, laughs as we do.

How do we know God looks like that? The Book God wrote tells us that God created humans in his own image, in the image of God created he him; male and female created he them. Therefore human beings look like God because He formed them so, and they are His children. Each human person embodies male and female elements just like God does Himself. Since He made humans in His Image, we must look like Him, and He must look like us.

God is All. Some aspects of God's Beingness:
God is 'Alpha' and 'Omega' – 'Beginning' and 'End', Eternal; Forgiving; Glorious; Holy; Incorruptible; Immortal; Invisible; Light; Immutable – unchangeable; Just; Kind; Merciful; Most High; Omnipotent – All powerful; Omniscient - All seeing; Only Wise; Past finding out; Perfect; Power; Our Rock, Timeless; Unsearchable.

Where did God the Father live before the foundation of the World?
God lives in one place in His Heaven, however God's Holy Spirit Power is also Omnipresent and everywhere, and **everything** that exists is an expression of that Power.

God is Eternal, is not bound by Time, He is an Invisible 'Spirit', and has 'always' lived in an 'unseen' Spiritual dimension, a 'Heaven' where He has His Throne. We have no way of knowing 'where' that was originally, or indeed if it was a 'where'.

God had a Plan to extend Himself into a Family. That Plan involved the creation of another Being.

CHAPTER 2

GOD CREATED HIS SON – THE WORD

In a 'timeless beginning', God became the 'Father' when He created His Son, the Word, from God's own Spirit Matter. There is only One God, and He created His Son from His Own Spirit Essence, and thus the Godhead became a family of two, God the Father and His Son who was the Word which together were and are One God.

The Word, His Son, who God appointed **heir** of all things, by whom also he made the worlds; Everything was Created by the Word, for by him were all things created, that are in heaven, and that are in Earth, visible and invisible, whether they be thrones, or dominions, or principalities, or powers: <u>all</u> **things were created by Him, and for Him:**

GOD IS TIMELESS - AND HUMANS ARE BOUND TO THINK IN TIME

'Before' and 'after' are not words we can really use when talking about God and the Word His Son, because they are timeless. Humans are bound into the concept of 'time', but they cannot explain 'time' as it is a Spiritual Power of God. Part of God wanted to form a Family of Beings.

THE PLANNING PHASE OF GOD AND HIS SON The formation & Development of 'The Plan of God'

There is no record of 'when' our timeless God created His Plan. With God there is no time, but for humans to think of things or events happening without including the element of 'time' is difficult to do. So we can imagine that His Plan was devised over 'timeless aeons' and further defined together with his Son, the Word.

The incredible complexity of God's plan

These 'aeons' of developing God's Plan included the design of DNA, the key to all the myriad variety of all the Earthly animal fauna, flora and human beings in all their complexity. The crowning part of His Plan concerned how humans would eventually become an integral part of the Greater Family of the Children that God is Creating.

'Then' God began an indeterminate period of planning during 'eonian times' however long that was. But as humans, we can only imagine anything in the context of what we know as 'time', that 'before' God created 'time', God the Father and the Word who are One, explored the concepts and design of everything spiritual and physical that we are aware of now **_before_** any of what we know existed in those two forms of life.

It was the 'time' when God was working with His Created Son and instructing the Word in the matters concerning the 'how's' of all the detailed plans that were to be involved with the Creation of all things by the Word. Which first included all spiritual beings, and then all the physical matter of the entire universe.

Everything on Earth, in the heavens, and the universe, physical and spiritual were planned in every detail before they were Created. This included the creation of DNA, that awesome spiral from which all the millions of species of flora, the plants, the trees; the fauna, animals, fish and birds, a million types of insects, and a trillion types of bacteria. The pinnacle of all was the Creation of human beings which They planned, and who were designed, ultimately to become God and part of Themselves.

During this planning 'time', another almost incomprehensible part of God's Plan, that is virtually unknown by anyone in the world of 'Churchianity' was discussed in Heaven by God and His Son before the Creation of all things.

The Plan included the incredible fact that God's Son the Word, at a specific 'time' in history, would give up His awesome position of Power in the Godhead, and become a man and be willing to die for the whole human race. The enormity and extent of this sacrifice is something that very few have understood, but now some who are reading this may begin to have more appreciation for what was done for humanity by our God.

One cannot even begin to imagine the complexity of creating all the designs involved in the Plan. The expanse of the expanding universe is beyond our comprehension, yet God has a name for every heavenly body, and calls them all by name.

Ancient writings penned millennia ago say God stretches (expands) out the north over the empty place, and hangs the Earth upon nothing. In the same texts a word speaking of the heavens being 'formed' actually means a twisting motion. Galaxies are now observed to be spirals like many sea shells.

In another search to explain 'energy', in 1998 some scientists discovered that the universe is not only expanding but that its expansion is accelerating. The leading theory to explain the accelerating expansion is the existence of a *hypothetical* repulsive force called 'dark energy'. They say 'dark energy' may *possibly* be composed of some so far undiscovered subatomic particles which accounts for 85% of the matter in the universe, and about a quarter of its total energy density.

Although modern physics now proposes that the Universe is expanding, this is apparently contradicted by the notion that 'gravity' actually pulls everything together, and would slow expansion down. So some suggest that 'dark energy' is actually a kind of "antigravity" that pushes the universe apart more strongly than gravity pulls it together.

Now 'black holes' have been 'discovered' where gravity is so strong that nothing can escape out of them. 'Worm holes' are another conjecture, and are thought to exist due to a twisting action of some kind.

There is apparently no end to human attempts to explain the inexplicable. However God's Secret Powers are all beyond our human understanding.

How is it that the Earth stays in its orbit where it is with such precision? Should we really put this down to the random effect of 'Gravity' on the forming of our Planet since the 'Big Bang'? Or just admit that something as precise as this needed to be Designed?

Humans continue to wrestle with some of the mysteries they have uncovered in the search for ever more knowledge. Of black holes, dark energy, the red shift, the rate of expansion of the Universe. So many 'theories', ideas, guesses that are not facts, and so very little appreciation of the awesome Powers of the Creator.

Think about the creation of the DNA spiral, that amazing 'framework' of all living things. The unimaginable work involved with use of that 'framework' in the design of millions of species, all intertwined in the unbelievably complicated and yet delicate ecological balance that enabled all to reproduce, and were part of the food chain which ensured all were fed, yet all maintained in a balance without any one species dominating the entire world. It is a fact that the weight of insects is greater than all the people in the world. Good job their numbers are under control!

Just these few details outlined here must have involved an almost infinite complexity of interdependent design. That is a mind-stopping thought in itself.

All this complexity without a Designer?

Everything that is made by human beings begins its life as a mental thought, then a picture is built up in the mind of the person. As this picture develops, the design is perfected. Then the materials and methods involved in the physical production of the design are carefully planned. Nothing we know of in our human world ever came to exist without a designer and a manufacturer,

Yet many in the 'scientific' world argue endlessly that there was no 'Designer' of our fabulous Universe, our incredible Solar system, our Earthly home, or our human minds; no 'Manufacturer', 'it all just happened over billions of years all by itself'.

If anyone suggested that the watch on my wrist, that chair, or that motor car, or that jet plane 'just happened', everyone would think they were crazy, mad, or insane. People around hearing that statement would probably send for the men in white coats to take them away.

What a tragedy it is, that so many very highly 'educated' people accept the **theory** of evolution, or state that 'everything came from nothing', and thereby commit 'sacrilege', which is defined as 'stealing credit from God'.

'After' God and the Word 'completed' their Planning and Design, the Father appointed the Word to be His Chief Executive Officer, and to be the actual Creator of all things, and ultimately Heir of all things. 'All things' were not created from nothing, they were Created from God's Spirit Matter Power. The Word would use all God the Father's Secret, Invisible Powers like His Spirit Power, 'Gravity', Centrifugal Force, Magnetism, Mathematics, the 'Electromagnetic Spectrum', the periodic Table of Elements, and many other of His Powers to Create all things.

CHAPTER 3

THEN GOD THE WORD BEGAN TO CREATE ALL THINGS

For by him, the 'Word' were all things created, that are in heaven, and that are in Earth, visible and invisible, whether they be thrones, or dominions, or principalities, or powers: all things were created by the Word, and for him:

It is only by reason of 'Faith', which is a spiritual gift from God given to those He chooses, that some 'few' can even begin to understand how the galaxies, stars, planets and the world were produced and framed in their specific positions in the universe by the Word of God, and that things which are 'seen' were assembled, constructed, made and formed out of and from invisible matter which cannot be seen.

Notice, the Word created all that is visible to us, but also He created all those spirit principalities and powers that are invisible to us.

First, the Word created Invisible Spirit Beings, Lucifer, & God's Spirit Being Sons

God the Father gave of His Spirit Matter and Essence to His Son to create Spirit beings. Before the Word created the physical heavens and the Earth, He, the Word, created other spirit beings, the many 'principalities and powers'. The Word tells us that He also created other 'sons of God'.

These 'sons of God' and other angelic beings were present later at the time of the subsequent creation of the physical heavens and the Earth, they sang and shouted with joy at the incredible spectacle. Who were these 'sons of God'? What were their activities in the past? And what are they doing now? This is covered later.

God Creates Spiritual Good and Evil

Part of the Plan of God was for the Word to create a Spirit Being who would become Satan the Adversary which He did. Why did God do that? It is a part of our Father's Wisdom concerning His Plan. God is Love and Satan embodies all that is the opposite of Love.

Without light we cannot understand darkness. Without silence, we cannot appreciate sound. So without knowing 'evil', we would never be able fully to comprehend 'good'.

God formed the light, and created darkness: He made peace and good, and the opposite. This truth may present difficulties for many 'religious' people who do not allow God's Word the Bible to lead their minds into a true understanding of God.

God created good and evil, and God the Father is in complete charge and firmly in control of the entire creation, the 'good' the 'bad' and the 'ugly'.

This explains the answer to the question so many have in their minds. "How can a God of Love allow all the horrendous evil that exists in this world?"

The experience of the horrors of this present evil world is a vital part of God's Plan to show human beings the awful result of breaking His Laws of Love. This is an essential part of human life which will ultimately lead each person to appreciate the Love of God and the vast extent and glorious natture of His Plan for all His children.

Throughout history, invisible Satan and his unseen spiritual cohorts have always been, and still are at every level of government of the Earth. Satan has managed to convince the whole world that he does not exist. How clever is that? He and his demons are still hard at work to influence and lead people astray, and to encourage them to break the Laws of Love. They subtly cause almost all people on Earth to ignore God in their lives, and to follow their own nature and lusts. Human beings have to learn that to break the Laws of Love will always cause terrible suffering.

God uses 'evil' to bring about the 'good' of His loving purposes. God does not 'sin' in the use of evil. He can use His laws in whatever manner He chooses to achieve His ultimate aims. God has the Authority to use evil for good, but this option is not open to human beings. We cannot fathom this with our human minds, but if there had been a 'better' way to achieve His purpose, we have to trust that God would have done it differently.

God knew from before the 'beginning' that having a Family would involve enormous suffering. Human beings are made in God's image, and He built into us that same desire He has, to make a family. To have a family, people are willing to go ahead and to endure the pain of childbirth, and despite the fact that parents know full well that bringing up children will inevitably involve a lot of emotional and even physical pain as they grown up for both them and their children, but still that does not deter men and women from that purpose. God is the same way.

God's Secret Creative Powers were then used by the Word to form all things visible.
God gave the Word, His Son a 'portion' of His Spirit Matter and His Unseen Powers of Light, Gravity, Centrifugal Force, Magnetism, Electricity, Radiation, Capillary Attraction and so

on, and gave all His Secret types of Energy to His Son from which to Create all things.

At the Father's direction, the Word then created space, the physical heavens, Galaxies without number, the Earth and its Solar system, all by using God's Invisible Secret Powers of Creation.

Then the Word created everything inanimate, all matter like the periodic table of elements, the gases, liquids and solids like rock, all were created by the Word, and everything is continually empowered by God's Invisible Powers. Everything that is 'animate', everything that lives, has inherent 'Life-Force', one of the Spiritual Powers and Gifts of God.

Scientists know the existence of these powers of Gravity, Centrifugal Force, the Electromagnetic Spectrum, Magnetism, Radiation, etc., but they call them 'The Laws of Physics'.

This is pure 'sacrilege', which means they are literally stealing the credit for the Design and the Act of Creation from God who used these Powers to create all we know. These secret powers belong to God. They are in existence forever and are used by the Word, who became Jesus Christ, continually to uphold and sustain the Universe.

The Three 'Heavens' of the Bible

The Word Created the heavens and the Earth. There are three 'heavens' mentioned in the Bible

The first 'heaven', is the sky where the birds and planes fly in the atmosphere surrounding the Earth; then there is the second 'heavens' where countless galaxies are spread across the universe which is constantly expanding. These are the physical 'heavens'.

There is nothing in His Word to tell us where God lived before He Created His Son, and appointed Him Creator and Heir of All Things, but since He is Spirit, His dwelling place is in the 'third heaven' the Spiritual Realm that is invisible to human beings, which may well be closer than we think.

The Energy of and within matter
Einstein's 'Theory of Relativity' can only be really understood by one who has studied advanced mathematics, but even then they must remember that it is just a 'theory'. Theories are simply 'guesses', which at best are all assumptions, conjectures, hypotheses, and suppositions. Many take Einstein's ideas as a basis from which to form yet more 'theories', although others question as to whether or not they are true.

But we can learn something about the Awesome Power of God from Einstein's work. Even if his theory is not entirely accurate, some knowledge of his notions can give astonishing insight into the awesome Power of our Creator.

Mathematics is a Power of God
Incidentally, what we call 'mathematics' is actually another one of the mysteries of God. The 'laws of maths' are really one branch of the Laws of God. God used His Laws of Mathematics to create the universe and all things in it. The incredible patterns that exist in numbers formed by those laws are not just 'there', they were designed to be there. We can use them, we can even think we understand them, but how they are the way they are is another mystery.

But why are there 'prime numbers'? The first five prime numbers are: 2, 3, 5, 7 and 11, there are many more. A prime number is a whole number that has only two factors — 1 and itself. Put another way, a prime number can be divided evenly only by 1 and by itself. Prime numbers also must be greater than 1.

Why is there what is called the 'Fibonacci' sequence, such that each number is the sum of the two preceding ones, starting from 0 and 1. The first few are 0, 1, 1, 2, 3, 5, 8, 13, 21, 34, 55... This pattern continues ad infinitum. Mathematicians can work out the sequence of these numbers, but they cannot explain how they came to be.

New Geometry reveals another aspect of God's Powers.
Geometry is another branch of mathematics which until recently was entirely based on books written by the Greek Euclid in 300B.C. Geometry is a branch of mathematics concerned with whole shapes of one, two and three dimensions, like a line, triangles and cubes; and the size, relative position of figures, and the properties of space.

In the last century, many explored a new concept of shapes and dimensions concerning the possibility that the three dimensional world we think we live in may have a 4_{th} or 5_{th} or more. Also that the number expressing the dimension of shapes could be a fraction rather than a whole number. Fundamental suppositions of the centuries old accepted 'rules' of geometry were being challenged.

Observations of apparently chaotic shapes and patterns in nature and even in our business world led to further research. The shape of coastlines, trees, surfaces of broken rocks, frequency of earthquakes, floods, even market prices over long periods, all seemed to occur with a 'regular irregularity'. Was there a principle of order within the chaos observed that could be discovered?

After some years of research by many Geometers, in 1975, the word 'Fractal' was coined by a Frenchman. The word means 'self-similar but different'. The new word 'Fractal' was coined to embrace a totally new concept of shapes.
Before that moment of geometric discovery equations were painstakingly solved one at a time, but now shapes might

be defined by repeating a fractional equation in a feedback loop. The concept behind it opened up a completely new field of Geometry.

It is now clear that the physical realm is structured along the lines of fractal geometry. Mathematicians had discovered another of God's Invisible Laws. Fractals are common in the natural world and are found nearly everywhere. An example is broccoli. Every branch of broccoli looks just like its parent stalk, but microscopically different. The surface of the lining of your lungs has a fractal pattern that allows for more oxygen to be absorbed. Such complex real-world processes can now be expressed in equations through fractal geometry.

No two identical snowflakes have ever been observed among countless numbers examined, all similar but different. 'Gazillions' of pebbles and sand particles on the beaches, no two the same. DNA is another example of a 'pattern' that is always similar, yet contains an infinite number of irregularities. Put simply there are no two humans, cows, frogs, or any other creature that are the same in every respect.

When God Creates He reveals a part of His Nature that is 'Fractal', in that there are no two things exactly the same in Creation but are 'similar'. How wonderful is that?

For thousands of years, mathematicians with all their brain power have only been able to make one calculation at a time. With the recent development of computing power, humans can now make billions of calculations a second.

The Mind of God who designed and 'Is' the Laws of Mathematics has always had the Power to make an infinite number of calculations simultaneously for Eternity. Awesome.

How much energy did it take to create the Universe?

Einstein's Theory (guess.) of Relativity is expressed as $e=mc^2$ where e is energy, m is mass, and c^2 is the speed of light squared.

Simply stated, it suggests that it takes an almost unbelievably vast amount of energy to make a very small amount of matter. The energy inside the atom is huge, as witnessed when the power of an atomic or Hydrogen bomb is released from just a few grams or ounces of a uranium isotope.

From our knowing this, when God through the Word created all the Matter there is, we could deduce that it must have taken more Energy to do so than it is possible for humans to count or express in any terms. God is the source of all energy. When all this fantastic amount of energy was released at the time of Creation, perhaps there was a 'Big Bang', but who knows?

Humans have never really understood where the energy that sustains the rotation of particles 'inside' each atom comes from. They cannot because it is one of God's secret things. The electromagnetic spectrum may be observed in action and used in many ways, but it is still a mystery.

Only a few decades ago previous scientific thought suggested that there were three basic subatomic particles: Electrons, protons, and neutrons. With the advent of the electron microscope and other amazing devices like the new huge particle accelerators, more particles were 'discovered'. Scientists now grapple with many 'new' particles they have 'discovered' which of course have been there all the time. The more 'scientists' probe into the minutiae of matter the more they discover about God's incredible Mind, but they will never be able to understand it completely.

The Cosmos - the universe as a system with an order and pattern

God and His Son created the heavens, the Universe: For by him were all things created, that are in heaven, and that are in Earth, visible and invisible, whether they be thrones,

WHO and WHAT IS GOD?

or dominions, or principalities, or powers: all things were created by him, and for him, and they are all similar and different.

These are the generations or history of the heavens and of the earth when they were created, in the day that the Lord God made the earth and the heavens.

In the original descriptive language of the manuscripts it becomes apparent that the origin of the universe was a progression. First everything was 'made', then 'created', and then 'formed'. Everything was 'made' or gathered together, then 'created' in its original form, then 'formed' much like a potter makes a pot.

Our solar system was designed to provide the environment the Earth would need in order for it to be inhabited.

There are various theories and estimates as to when the universe began, and how long it took, but all these ideas are just that. Recent discoveries put old ideas into a different perspective.

Only a generation ago, the scientific belief of the time stated categorically that there was only one Galaxy, the one in which we live. It was called the Milky Way. Some say it gets its name from a Greek myth about the goddess Hera who sprayed milk across the sky. Like many words we use today, the English name of our galaxy is derived from its Latin name: Via Lactea. Translated, that means "the road of milk."

When we gaze up at the night sky with the naked eye, on a clear night the band of light across it does look 'milky' because so many of the stars in it are so small they appear to us as a milky fog. The Romans actually got the name from the Greeks, who called our galaxy "galaxias kyklos" or "milky circle". It is said to have a radius of 52,850 light years, and contain 250 billion stars, or 150 billion give or take a billion or so, and more in a diameter of twice that!

Since the invention of ever bigger telescopes, including the Hubble and Webb Telescopes which are outside our atmosphere in space, and thereby provide a much clearer view of the universe through 360° in all directions, scientists have had continually to revise their understanding of the Cosmos. It is now thought that there are as many Galaxies as there are stars in the Milky Way. God's cosmos got larger?

A light year is about 9.5 trillion kilometres or 5.9 trillion miles. It is the distance that light travels in vacuum in one Julian year (365.25 days). A 'Light year' is nothing but the distance (it is said that it is not a measure of time) that the light travels in one year. The closest two main twin stars to the Earth are Alpha Centauri A and Alpha Centauri B, and are an average of 4.3 light-years from Earth.

So, when 'Theoretical Astro-Physicists' talk about the universe being about 13.7 billion years old, and say that light reaching us from the earliest known galaxies has been travelling, for more than 13 billion year, are they contradicting the definition of a Light year which is the distance with the time? Are we at all sure that all that information is actually factual, or are scientists going to find out over time how wrong they may have been in their calculations? This has certainly been true of the journey of scientific 'discoveries' over the last couple of centuries.

Our Solar System is different and very special

Scientists are often heard to 'surmise', which means 'to suppose that something is true without having evidence to confirm it', that because the numbers of Galaxies and stars is so 'astronomical' (pun intended) it is thought a virtually 'mathematical certainty' that there are, and indeed 'must be', other places in the Universe where Life like ours exists. It is clear that this is pure conjecture.

Of all the Astro-physicists interviewed in a special programme about 'SETI', the 'Search for Extra-Terrestrial Intelligence', not one of those scientists even mentioned or referred to a 'Greater Power' or God. Without exception, they were all of the so far unsupported opinion that we are not 'alone' in the Universe. Some voiced the notion that inside all human beings there is a desire for that 'feeling' to be true, and that there is 'someone' out there. NASA even includes records of sounds and music in their space probes. This 'feeling' of 'alone-ness' is partly what gave rise to the billions spent on 'SETI', the Search for Extra-Terrestrial Intelligence.

The fact is, it is almost certainly true that at some level most people do feel 'alone'; and that 'feeling' is part of the make-up of the mind and spirit of human beings, and that it was put there by God. Why? Because God wants us to search for Him, and to seek Him. This is because at some level the 'god-part' of us wants to unite with our Creator. What a pity it is that all those involved with SETI are looking in the wrong direction. **<u>God *Is* the Extra-Terrestrial Intelligence our inner 'soul' is seeking, and clear evidence of His Intelligence is right here on the Earth all the time.</u>**

The Earth was formed to be inhabited.
The Lord that created the heavens states: God himself that formed the Earth and made it; He established it, he created it not in vain, He formed it to be inhabited: I am the Lord; and there is none else.

There is no suggestion or evidence that any other part of the heavenly host of the Cosmos was formed to be inhabited and lived on. When we understand what God is doing here, and how special our 'life' is to Him, this clearly is His Unique Project. It is much more probable that this Earth is the only place in the Universe upon which God has bestowed the mysterious gift of 'Life'.

The design of our Solar System and the Earth

The Sun is 864,400 miles (1,391,000 kilometres) across, and about one hundred times the diameter of Earth. It is so large that about 1,300,000 planet Earths could fit inside it.

There are eight planets in the Solar System, which are at an increasing distance from the Sun: Mercury, Venus, Earth, Mars, Jupiter, Saturn, Uranus, and Neptune.

The Sun's heat and radiation are immense. Earth is about *94.5 million miles (152 million km),* from the Sun. If there were not protective layers between the Sun and the Earth, everything would burn up. Sunlight takes eight minutes to arrive at the Earth and provides the energy and warmth needed for life to exist. The Earth's orbit around the Sun is oval or elliptical. Because the Earth is tilted slightly, the amount of sunlight reaching the Earth varies and gives us the seasons, and an annual sense of time during a lifetime.

God Created Time

When God designed the Earth and miraculously caused it to rotate at a constant precise speed every twenty-four hours, more accurately than even the most advanced clocks humans can make, He Created 'night and days'. The orbiting Moon to give us 'months', and our annual orbit around the Sun to give us 'years'. By these things God implanted a vital sense of 'Time' into all life on Earth. The seasonal life of plants, the migration of animals and birds, and the length or duration of 'Life' itself are all determined by the sense of 'Time'. God has given us 'Time' which is a Spiritual matter, and therefore not to be fully understood.

Chapter 4

THEN GOD REFORMED THE EARTH TO MAKE IT HABITABLE FOR HIS CHILDREN

We are told plainly the Lord created the heavens and the Earth; God himself that formed the Earth and made it and established it. We are clearly told that He formed it to be **inhabited**, according to His Plan.

We really do not know when the Earth was first formed. There are estimates, but can anyone really know? Certainly it was clearly a very long time ago as we measure time.

The Word of God, the Bible which is truth, provides us with the true record of the generations of the heavens and of the earth when they were created, in the day, or at the time that the Lord God made the Earth and the heavens.

In its 'beginning' the Earth is described as being almost without form, covered in water and darkness, probably because of the dust and debris surrounding it. There is still a lot of 'debris' in space, asteroids, meteorites and 'dust'. God began His work of reforming it.

God began to reform and mould the Earth's land and the seas were and are contained by its shores except when storms and cyclones occur, which when you ponder about that, it is amazing. The waters of the sea evaporate, form clouds, and the snow, rain and dew provide pure distilled water. God populated Earth with all the fauna and flora, and everything that would be needed to provide a perfect home for human beings was completed in just six days. Please do not just dismiss or reject this statement. God does not lie, a day is a day in this instance.

Carefully examine the 'days' of creation, and it immediately becomes apparent that those 'days' could not be thousands or millions of years. All the different plants and creatures on the Earth are part of an intricately balanced ecological system. If the different species of plants, insects and animals of that system came into being separately over aeons of time, pollination could not have occurred and the balance of all life on Earth as we know it could not have existed.

God the Word reformed the Earth to be inhabited in six days.
The inspired record tells how the Spirit of God the Word 'moved' upon the face of the waters. The Hebrew word here for 'moved' included the sense of brooding, moving in a caring relaxed way to clean up and clear the atmosphere that surrounds our Planet. The air was cleared and was adjusted to contain the perfect balance of Nitrogen, Oxygen and trace element gases for all air breathing life on Earth.

So the first thing God did in the reformation of Earth was to Create Light.

Day One. God created light. He is Light
God is Love and Light, and in Him is no darkness at all.

The very first thing God did through the Word was to create 'light' and banish the darkness by clearing the atmosphere of debris. By creating 'light' on the Earth God was putting His Power and Presence here. The 'Light' enables our eyes to see and appreciate all the incredible design and beauty of everything He made in glorious colours. Sight is truly a miraculous gift to His children. Also the invisible infra-red frequencies of Light provide the warmth and the heat that are essential to life on this planet.

The Sun and the Moon 'create' our day and night as the Earth rotates.

So what is light? Is it a wave, a particle, photons, and have other elements? Or is light all of those and more? Does light only travel in straight lines, or can it bend with the influence of other Powers of God? Some suggest that it does.

Light is a tiny window, the visible part of the entire electromagnetic spectrum which is largely an invisible Energy. It exists from below the lowest frequencies of sound up to the highest frequencies, to the shorter wavelengths of ultraviolet light, and above that of dangerous x-rays and lethal gamma rays.

Without the light and heat of the Sun, life on Earth would be impossible. But part of the light of the Sun consists of frequencies that are lethal to Life, and Life on Earth has to be shielded from that part.

The Earth's magnetosphere, its magnetic field and other layers, protect us here on Earth from the effects of the plasma, the deadly ionised gas of the Sun's 'flares', and blocks it safely from reaching the surface of our planet. The sun gives off a great deal of bands of radiation that would destroy life on Earth were it not for the ozone and other layers. How amazing are God's Works.

The notion put forth by many modern 'scientific' communities that humans could establish a home on other planets in our Solar system that have environments totally hostile to life is completely ludicrous. There is a lot of talk nowadays about 'terraforming' or making Earth on Mars and transporting millions there from Earth. This is a truly nonsensical idea since the radiation levels on Mars, which is not protected like the Earth is, would 'fry' humans in an instant even if they were protected to some degree by their space suits.

We have everything we need to enjoy a wonderful life here on Earth, but clearly, we are failing miserably to do this even though we have, or did have perfect conditions. As a result of the ways we have misused the fauna, flora, and mineral wealth, it appears now that we have damaged our environment beyond repair. Not content with that, we think about how we can get to another planet and will then no doubt proceed to spoil that place too.

Day Two. God divided the waters and made the 'firmament' the land

The word 'firmament' means expanse of the land including the arch of the sky. God divided the waters that are above the land in the sky, and the waters on the Earth, and the waters that are under the land. A picturesque description of the reality we know.

God called the dry land earth, and the gathering together of the waters He called Seas. The seas are another miracle. They are contained by the sandy shores of the Earth. Amazing how the particles of all the sand are much the same size. Sand is not broken down rock over billions of years, it was made that way.

God also created the Moon to be exactly the right size and placed it at precisely the right distance from the Earth so that its gravitational pull would cause the oceans to be tidal. Twice each day, the entire seas of our Planet move back and forth which is essential for the health of the life of the sea.

The seas are a solution of just the right amount of salt which is a purifier. The seas contain abundant life in many forms and the salt and the motion of the seas keeps the seas 'alive' and prevents the waters becoming putrid. Anyone who has taken home some sea water with little crabs and tiny fish knows the disappointment of how quickly the life dies, and the water begins to stink. The way God created movement of the seas ensured that all the life in it would survive. Tragically human activities are now progressively 'killing' the seas.

The seas also provide the miracle of fresh water as vapour rises from the sea and creates clouds which release purified distilled water in little droplets of rain. Rain becomes streams and rivers that beautify all the country through which they run, and then flow into the sea.

This we all know but mostly take for granted, however this process is a miracle that enables 'life' on our Earthly home. Apart from some bacteria, none of the flora and fauna on Earth can live without that pure water

Pure water also enables cleanliness and hygiene. Many people around the world collect rain and store it in tanks. Why is that not common practice, and built into all new homes? Where millions in many countries have abundant water clean enough to drink, they waste trillions of gallons every day by flushing it down toilets. Some countries have learned that it is perfectly possible to make odourless dry toilets which breakdown human waste into a usable product.

Where greedy humans have made huge dams, they stop the natural flow of pure water, and thereby steal it from those who would benefit downstream. This causes another serious problem. Dams stop the natural rise and flow of water during the seasons causing rivers and streams to stagnate. Pure water has to flow or it 'dies'. It grows green algae which take all the oxygen out of the water and the fish and all life in it dies. This is happening wherever dams exist.

Tragically where water is scarce on Earth, there is a lack of cleanliness and hygiene, so diseases flourish. If humans really cared for one another this need not be the case at all.

Day Three. God Created grass, herbs, trees

The records tells how God had designed, formed and prepared all the varieties of flora, the plants and the trees before they were ever put into the ground by Him. It says that God made every plant of the field *before* it was put into the earth, and every herb of the field *before* it grew: for the Lord God had not caused it to rain upon the earth, and there was not yet a man to till the ground. But there went up a mist from the earth, and watered the whole face of the ground. All this work was prepared before God created Adam.

Seeds found stored in the pyramids for thousands of years still contained that miracle of 'life'. When discovered and were sown, they sprouted and produced healthy plants. The miracle of 'life' encapsulated in seed should cause us to praise God.

To confound those who deny Creation, seeds often have two or three protective coatings, and for this to have occurred spontaneously by itself is clearly impossible. Also that trees yielded fruit whose seed was inside it, another incredible design feature.

All the plants and trees were to reproduce themselves 'after their kind'. We know the utter reliability that all seeds will reproduce the plants they came from. Animals also reproduce after their 'kind', birds make birds, fish make fish, dogs make dogs, elephants make elephants, monkeys make monkeys, and humans make humans. Each can produce a number of varieties within species, but they are still birds, fish, dogs, elephants, monkeys and humans.

There is no record whatsoever of one species morphing into another. This is another unsubstantiated fabrication of proponents of the evolutionary theory.

Even Darwin himself was plagued with serious doubts until his death because he could not reconcile the problem of the design he observed in all things as opposed to his idea that they all occurred spontaneously of their own accord. The 'theory' remains a 'theory' a guess, and unproven idea, yet it is believed to be **fact** by intelligent people. When the subject comes up almost everyone seems to have an almost religious fervour, an intense and passionate feeling about evolution.

God had substantially now created the fauna and flora, but the next day brought the wonderful mechanism by which everything lives and grows.

Day four. God created 'lights', day and night, seasons, days and years

So, God organised the Earth to be at a certain tilt and to rotate so that the Sun and the Moon would produce days, months and seasons. God said in His own language, 'Let there be lights in the firmament of the heaven to divide the day from the night; and let them be for signs, and for seasons, and for days, and years: And let them be for lights in the firmament of the heaven to give light upon the earth: and it was so. And God made two great lights; the greater light to rule the day, and the lesser light to rule the night: he made the stars also. And God set them in the firmament of the heaven to give light upon the earth, and to rule over the day and over the night, and to divide the light from the darkness: and God saw that it was good'.

Day five. God made all the creatures that have life

And God said, Let the waters bring forth abundantly the moving creature that hath life, and fowl that may fly above the earth in the open firmament of heaven. And God created great whales, and every living creature that moves, which the waters brought forth abundantly, after their kind, and every winged fowl after his kind: and God saw that it was good. And God blessed them, saying, Be fruitful, and multiply, and fill the waters in the seas, and let fowl multiply in the earth. And God said, Let the earth bring forth the living creature after his kind, cattle, and creeping thing, and beast of the earth after his kind: and it was so. And God made the beast of the earth after his kind, and cattle after their kind, and everything that creeps upon the earth after his kind: and God saw that it was good.

Everything was to produce offspring after their 'kind' or 'genus'. A **genus** can include more than one species. When biologists talk about a **genus**, they mean one or more species of animals or plants that are closely related to each other. No genus or species can change into another. And so it is to this day.

And the evening and the morning were the fifth day.

Day Six. Then the Word Created the Human Man and the Woman

And God said, Let us *make* man in our image, after our likeness: The phrase 'let us' implies that there was communication and discussion between the Father and the Son when the time came to begin to make their first children.

The word in Hebrew translated 'make' is 'asah', literally to do or make, in the broadest sense to accomplish, to bring forth, The next part of the record says God *'created'* man in His own image. In the image of God created He him, male and female created He them. This word 'created' in Hebrew is 'bara' to create, select or feed.

And then further detail adds that God *formed* man of the dust of the *ground* and breathed into him the breath of life. The Hebrew word for formed is *yatsar*, to press, to squeeze into shape); to mould into a form; especially as a potter; figuratively, to fashion, frame, make. And the word *ground* in Hebrew is *adamah* meaning red soil, or clay, country, earth, ground, husband(-man) husbandry, land, hence the name Adam.

God then formed Adam perfectly in every detail of his structure, his bones, his muscles, his sinews, and all his organs including the heart, liver, the spleen, the kidneys, the intestines, and so on. His mind that can think and plan and create which are Godly powers, the digestive system, and even the discrete design of the waste disposal system. Now we understand quite a lot about how the human body works, and wonder at its amazing complexity. This gives us an opportunity for daily appreciation and thanks to God.

God formed man of the dust of the ground, and breathed into his nostrils the breath of life; and man became a living soul or being. As already stated, human beings are made in God's image, in His form and shape. The word Hu-man is derived from an ancient word root where 'Hu' means God. So Humans are 'God-men' and women. In what sense are we 'God'? We are made in God's image, and we have the potential to join Him in His God Family one day.

At the end of some days of reformation, God says 'behold it was good'. However after the sixth day, God proclaims everything is 'very good'. Having made his first children, He is even more satisfied with His Work.

Virtually everyone has seen the series of pictures depicting the gradual development of hairy apes on all fours to a man standing upright with little hair on his body. These images are indelibly imprinted in our minds, but they are a tragic travesty, a perversion of the truth invented by God-rejecting people. The 'missing link' is still missing. They misrepresent what really happened in a false, absurd, and distorted way. In truth they are a horrific parody, a caricature with striking characteristics that ridicules and make a mockery of God's Creation of the first human beings.

Those pictures deny the magnificent Creation by God of Adam, the first human being. God created Adam, the first man, and he was perfect in every detail. The account tells of that creation in poetic language that is literal and figurative at the same time.

These words in bold are different in the original Hebrew language.

God **created** Adam from the 'dust of the ground'. It also says that God ***formed*** man of the dust of the ground, and breathed into his nostrils the breath of life; and man became a living soul or being.

In another account more information tells us that male and female created He them. God has male and female characteristics, and humans are created in God's image, therefore humans male and female embody both.

How are human beings exercising 'dominion' over God's Creation?

God said: And let them have ***dominion*** over the fish of the sea, and over the fowl of the air, and over the cattle, and over all the earth, and over every creeping thing that creeps upon the earth.

To have **dominion** over anything means being in charge of something or to rule it. Hundreds of English words contain the three letters 'dom'. Many have something to do with defining a type of or area of 'realm' or 'reign', such as domain, domestic, domicile, kingdom.

As with every other gift, human beings have a choice in regard to how they exercise that dominion. God wants his children to exercise loving, caring dominion over His Creation and 'dress it and keep it'. That phrase means to look after it carefully and well.

We were given dominion over the Earth to preserve the habitat of living creatures, not destroy it; to till the soil and build its 'heart', not pollute it with chemicals, herbicides, pesticides, poisons; to treat all animals with kindness and respect, not treat them harshly, be cruel and or terrify them when driving them with helicopters and quad bikes, house them in 'prisons' under awful conditions, feed them hormones, and other foodstuffs that are not suitable for them to eat; to treat the oceans with respect and enjoy the fishes of the sea, not dredge the sea of all its living creatures and throw much of it back dead, not pollute it with untreated sewage, nor dump millions of tons of plastic in them which endangers all marine life. What on God's Earth do we think we are doing?

God the Father has given Christ, Yahwh-Shua, dominion over the entire works of His hands, has put 'all things under his feet', or within His domain, and He is heir of all things. So how does Christ exercise that dominion? Does He control everything under His dominion? No, He does not. God and Christ wants every human being willingly to put themselves under their rule. God does not make us comply.

The 'Mind' of Christ Jesus give us our example of 'dominion'

The mind of Christ is summed up by: 'He who would be greatest of all, should be the servant of all'. Dominion is not about dominance, or rule by any type of pressure or force. It is based on the Law of Love. The ideal is for us to be in 'service' to everyone with Love, Respect, Consideration, Kindness, and Humility'. This is the Mind of Christ.

Everyone thinks about their own things, and that is good and right. However, everyone needs also to think, to consider and be aware of the needs and things of others. While taking proper care of ourselves, our daily focus is to emulate the Love of God and Christ to the maximum of our ability.

Most of humanity has lost sight of and respect for the God of Creation

It seems that most human beings have no shame when it comes to the way they abuse and mistreat this wonderful home called Earth. This is mainly because so few believe in or have any respect for the God of Creation who plainly is no longer in the hearts and minds of so many.

God is not far away, although we cannot see Him He is 'out there' and near to us. The solid evidence of His Reality is all around us here on Earth. God's invisible 'cloud' Heaven surrounds the physical Earth which is suspended within that 'cloud'. God's Life Power lives in us and we literally live in Him. "In Him, within His Power we live and move and have our being for we are His offspring", His children.

God's Life Power gives us every breath we breathe by activating the muscles of the diaphragm which draws air containing oxygen into our lungs. The miracle of God's Power energises the particles within each oxygen atom and causes them to rotate around the nucleus. The oxygen is separated from all the other gases in air, and it enters and vitalises the haemoglobin molecules in the blood.

Our 'Life' is in the blood.

The 'heme' molecule contains one iron atom, the bind point for oxygen. One oxygen molecule (O^2, or two oxygen atoms) binds to each iron atom via a covalent bond. Thus, each haemoglobin molecule is capable of carrying up to 4 oxygen molecules.

God's Life Power causes the muscles of the heart to contract and relax as it pumps the oxygenated blood around the body. Every heartbeat is a gift from God. All the blood is contained in blood vessels, and is not in the other tissues of the body. From the main arteries of the heart, the blood vessels divide up into smaller arteries, and then into tiny capillaries. Capillaries are so small that blood cells containing the life giving oxygen can only move through them one at a time.

Oxygen and food nutrients pass from these capillaries into the lymphatic system. The lymph bathes all the tissues of the body with oxygen and nutrients. And this is how oxygen gets into all the cells of the body and is used to generate the energy of life. The oxygen produces carbon dioxide as it 'burns' in the cells. The lymph picks up the carbon dioxide from the cells and it is reabsorbed from the lymph into the capillaries. The carbon dioxide is transferred into the lung tissues and breathed out.

There are twice as many lymphatic vessels in the lymphatic network as there are blood vessels, and twice as much lymph as blood in the body. About eight pints of blood and sixteen pints of lymph. The blood is pumped around the body by the heart. The lymph is circulated throughout the body by the movement of the muscles which surround the lymph vessels. This is why exercise is so very important for health.

The lymph also collects all the waste products from cell metabolism and renewal and transfers them to the main lymph drains in the neck. The waste is transferred into the blood circulation system for it to be filtered out and excreted by the kidneys. Marvellous are the works of God.

Human be-ings are god-men and women in a continuous state 'being-ness' or existing 'Life' with all these incredible bodily functions operating moment by moment until death.

How many people on this Earth think about the miracle of 'life' they have? Are they aware that every heartbeat is a continuous gift and an Act of God?

That every breath they take is also a continuous gift and an Act of God?

Day Seven. God finished the heavens and earth and rested from His work

Thus the heavens and the earth were finished, and all the host of them. And on the seventh day God ended His work which He had made; and He rested on the seventh day from all His work which he had made. And God blessed the seventh day, and sanctified it: because that in it He had rested from all his work which God created and made.

In the olden times people were very physical in outlook, and God gave them a set of laws which regulated their conduct. These laws had to be kept by His people on pain of death if they did not. The Sabbath days kept them in mind of God, and they needed the physical rest. The laws of what they could and not do on the Sabbath were very detailed and very restrictive.

After Christ, Yah-Shua the man came to Earth, He kept all those laws perfectly, paid the penalty for human sin, was resurrected and restored to His position with the Father in heaven,

He then sent God's Holy Spirit, the Comforter, to dwell in the minds of those who are the 'called'. The 'called' are not required to keep the physical laws, including the physical Sabbath, but to strive to keep the far more difficult Laws of the Spirit which include love, joy, peace, kindness, forgiveness, longsuffering, and all the fruits of the Spirit. Those who have God's Holy Spirit have entered into a different type of 'rest', a spiritual 'rest' which continues every day of the week.

God planted a garden in Eden

And the Lord God planted a garden for Adam eastward in Eden in the area of the Euphrates river; and there he put the man whom he had formed. And a river went out of Eden to water the garden.

In order to grow, plants and trees have to have water, but how do they draw water out of the Earth? It is by 'Capillary Attraction'.

CAPILLARY ATTRACTION DEFIES GRAVITY

Capillary attraction is yet another miraculous law of God's Power. What is capillary attraction? Capillary action is the ability of a liquid to flow in narrow spaces upwards in opposition to the external force of gravity.

When it rains (another miracle.), water soaks into the ground. But in addition to just retaining water, capillarity in soil also enables the horizontal and upward movement of water within the soil particles, as opposed to the downward movement caused by gravity. The smaller the soil porous texture, the higher the capillary rise in the water level.

Why is this such an important phenomenon? Because if this flow of liquids did not happen in this way, nothing would grow. Plants would not 'suck up' moisture from the soil against the force of gravity.

Transpiration is the process where plants and trees absorb water upwards against gravity by capillary attraction through the minute tubules in their roots and as water evaporates through the many pores on the leaf surface it makes room for more water to travel upwards. The rate of transpiration is directly related to the surface area of the leaves.

Through capillary action, trees draw water up through their roots and then up the tiny capillary layer all around the tree just under the bark of the trunk. A mature oak will transpire up to 50 gallons of water per day weighing around 500 pounds, which flow upwards to 80 feet or more up in the air against gravity. As the liquid vaporises and transpires through its leaves, more water is drawn up the trunk. Some huge trees transpire a great deal more. Amazing.

Those who deny the Designer can observe the way that Capillary Attraction works. Perhaps they may talk about surface tension and the meniscus effect, and so on, but how this Power happens against gravity is a miracle that scientists cannot explain at all.

Adam the gardener

And the Lord God took the man, and put him into the Garden of Eden that He had planted for him to dress it and to keep it.

And out of the ground in the garden the Lord God made every tree to grow that is pleasant to the sight, and good for food; the tree of life also in the midst of the garden, and the tree of knowledge of good and evil.

Then God gave Adam strict instructions concerning the trees in the garden. God's first generous statement was to tell Adam that he could freely eat of any and all the trees in the garden, except one. But of the tree of the knowledge of good and evil, God told Adam, you shall not eat of it:

for in the day that you eat of it you shall surely die. Adam must have understood that clearly. This instruction about the forbidden tree was given to Adam before Eve was formed.

God had another interesting job for Adam to do. God brought all the animals and birds to Adam for him to name them. And out of the ground the Lord God formed every beast of the field, and every fowl of the air; and brought them unto Adam to see what he would call them: and whatever Adam called every living creature that became its name.

So, Adam gave names to all cattle, and to the fowl of the air, and to every beast of the field; but for Adam among all the animals there was not found a helper that was suitable for him.

God Creates Eve
Then the Father said to the Word: It is not good that the man should be alone; I will make a suitable companion for him. And the Lord God caused a deep sleep to fall upon Adam, and he slept: and he took one of his 'ribs', and then closed up the flesh.

And the 'rib', or with whatever portion God had taken from Adam's body He made a woman, and brought her to the man. And Adam said, 'This is now bone of my bones, and flesh of my flesh: she shall be called Woman, because she was taken out of Man. And they were both naked, the man and his wife, and they were not at all ashamed'. And why would they be?

At that time, God explained to them the institution of marriage, for this reason a man will leave his father and his mother, and shall cleave unto his wife: and they shall be one flesh. No doubt God also explained to them all about the gift of sex in marriage.

WHO and WHAT IS GOD?

Marriage is certainly one of the most wonderful gifts that God has given to men and women. Historically many married people enjoyed a lifetime of mutual love, togetherness, respect and support. Sadly, that is becoming rare in the 'developed' countries. Tragically, Satan has been hard at work in our modern era to destroy that wonderful institution. More marriages are breaking down and couples are separating and getting divorced than ever before.

Even more tragically, the whole idea of marriage is losing popularity as more men and women 'get together' in a loose arrangement with virtually no commitment to one another. They live separate lives together, with separate bank accounts. It appears that no longer does a man consider it his privilege and duty to be the provider in the home.

In 1858 Emmeline Pankhurst started the women's rights movement to get the vote for women. In the '70's people used to talk of the 'Battle of the Sexes'. As time has gone on, because women have continued to be disrespected, been held back in business, and generally treated as second class citizens or worse, women have felt the need to continue the fight for 'equality'.

God wants all His children to love and respect each other. Satan wants to foment and stir up universal strife and discord. There should be no 'battle' between anyone, especially not between men and women. God does not want strife or disrespect between any, but in lowliness of mind, in humility He wants everyone to hold others in high esteem, and as being better than themselves.

Courtship used to follow a pattern. Two people attracted to each other spent time together. Then a period of 'courting' where sex before marriage was considered immoral and unacceptable. Then a couple would get 'engaged', save up for accommodation and plan their life together. When financially secure and able to maintain a home, only then would they consider starting a family.

The modern approach is different: Meet, have sex, get pregnant, have one or more babies, then perhaps think about getting married, or even then realise they do not like each other. God's precious gift has been ungratefully consigned to the bin. A travesty or what?

Now 'samesex' marriages are approved by some governments. In the past when Godless people experimented with sexual practices that are against natural law, they suffered extreme consequences. People may think they are free to behave as they wish with impunity, without any penalty, but time will tell.

One wonders how much sadness these behaviours and all of human rebellion causes our Father?

The knowledge of Good and Evil
The Lord God had planted a garden East of Eden. And out of the ground the Lord God made to grow every tree that is pleasant to the sight, and good for food; the tree of life also in the middle of the garden, and the tree of knowledge of good and evil.

And God said, Let us make man in our image, after our likeness: and let them have *dominion* over everything on Earth. When God formed the first man Adam, his work on Earth and that of all those who would follow was clearly defined. Then God gave His first commandments to Adam, spelling them out carefully. God gave Adam a job to do, not only to take good care of the garden He had planted but by extension the whole Earth, make it even more beautiful, and keep it in good condition. This responsibility is extended to all humans now living in the whole world who should have, and should now be, 'dressing and keeping' the whole world in good condition.

Rebellious, selfish, greedy humans are currently systematically destroying the fauna, flora, the climate and weather of our home, and even disturbing the fabric of the Earth's skin with 'fracking' and other mining practices.

Then God told Adam that it was not good for him to be alone, and that He would prepare a companion to be with him in his work. The Lord God caused a deep sleep to fall upon Adam, while he slept He took a part of Adam out of his body, and then closed up the flesh. From that part of Adam's body; God made a woman, and brought her unto the man.

Instead of enjoying and appreciating the story, many people scoff at the account of the Creation of Adam and Eve, even to the point of making the insane suggestion that everything came from 'nothing'. Those who reject God He calls fools.

God gave detailed instruction to the couple, how they would come together, become 'one flesh' and have children. God who is male and female is also One. And since God produced a Son, they are still One. So when a man and a woman become 'one', they are figuratively 'one' in the same way that God is One.

In human terms, we produce children during the loving God-given sex act which should be deeply revered, honoured, and respected. Sadly sex is far too often dragged into degradation by God rejecting people.

THE BIGGEST LIE – you shall not die

Satan in the form of the serpent was in the garden. Then in accordance with God's Plan for His children they have to come to know clearly the difference between 'good' and 'evil'. Here is how that lesson began.

Eve was walking alone in the garden and met Satan. Satan then told Eve the first and biggest lie, "If you eat of the fruit of the tree of the knowledge of good and evil, **You will not**

WHO and WHAT IS GOD?

die for God knows that in the day ye eat that fruit, then your eyes shall be opened, and ye shall be as gods, knowing good and evil".

The serpent was selling deceptive knowledge and false 'wisdom' by offering Eve the chance to be like God.

And when the woman saw that the tree was good for food, and that it was pleasant to the eyes, and a tree to be desired to make one wise, she took of the fruit and ate it, and gave also unto her husband with her; and ate some as well.

And the eyes of them both were opened, and they knew that they were naked; and they sewed fig leaves together, and made themselves aprons. Satan had begun his work of 'polluting' the purity of sex in their minds.

So Eve took of the fruit, ate some, and gave some to Adam who also ate the fruit. Adam knew full well that God had commanded him not to eat from that tree, but he gave in to the wishes and persuasion of his wife.

Later, God went looking for them in the garden but Adam and Eve were hiding because they knew they were naked and had disobeyed God and were afraid.

God found them, and to Eve He said, I will greatly multiply thy sorrow and your conception; in sorrow thou shall bring forth children; and your desire shall be to your husband, and he shall rule over you. And to Adam He said, Because you have listened to the voice of your wife, and have eaten of the tree of which I commanded you, saying, You shalt not eat of it: cursed is the ground for your sake; in sorrow shalt thou eat of it all the days of thy life; Thorns also and thistles shall it produce; and you shalt eat the herbs of the field; In the sweat of your face shall you eat bread, until you return unto the ground; for out of it you were taken: for dust you are, and unto dust you shall return.

And Adam called his wife's name Eve; because she was the mother of all living. Unto Adam also and to his wife did the Lord God make coats of skins, and clothed them. It is interesting that the record mentions that God made them clothing from the skins of animals.

So Adam and Eve knew the difference between Good and Evil
The Word God said to the Father: See, the man is become as one of us, to know good and evil: and now, in case he takes also of the tree of life, and eats from it, and gains eternal life for ever, We will expel him from the garden.

As a result of their rebellion the Lord God sent him forth from the Garden of Eden, to till the ground from whence he was taken. So God drove out the man; and he placed at the east of the garden of Eden Cherubims, and a flaming sword which turned every way, to keep the way of the tree of life.

The Truth about Life and Death
Satan's 'biggest lie' "You will not die" has two billion people in Christianity, and the rest in other religions on Earth fooled. They share a belief that when you die you are not dead, but go straight to 'heaven' or 'hell', or continue to exist in some other form.

The idea that we go to heaven when we die, or the concept of an ever burning hell (Dante's inferno) have no basis in the scriptures whatsoever. Hell is a notion that was thought up by religions to control people by holding them in perpetual fear if they did not meet the requirements of the church.

DEATH – when you die you are dead.
What then is the mechanism of life and death? God formed man of the dust of the ground, and breathed into his nostrils the breath of life and his human spirit; and man became a living soul.

Dust + Breath + Human Spirit = Living Soul
Living Soul - Breath - Human Spirit = Death & Dust

When the breath leaves the body the person is unconscious, unaware, and has ceased to exist as an entity. It is **not** living a 'floaty' existence in another dimension. The living know that they will die: but the dead know nothing. For in death the brain is dead so there can be no remembrance of anything.

All humans have a human spirit.
Humans have a hu-man, a god-man 'spirit' breathed into them with 'the breath of Life' at birth. This human spirit was designed so that God's children would be able to relate to and communicate with God via His Holy Spirit. When a human being dies, the human spirit returns to God who gave it. God stores this spirit until the time comes for that person to be resurrected to human life.

Human beings also have a carnal or fleshly human nature which is biased against God, and indeed at some level is at war with the God of Love. Of course all humans are capable of human love and affection, of kindness, and to a limited degree of exhibiting many of God's qualities.

The human spirit is also susceptible to suggestion and influences from Satan and his billions of cohorts. We have only to look at the horrendous, horrible activities of so many human beings on this Earth at this time to know that is true. Satanic inhumane activities are pandemic. Wars, criminal activities, rape, sexual degradation of all forms, torture, all the worst types of human's inhumanity to humans happen on a vast scale every day. Our rational minds can certainly see clearly the universal presence of evil at work all around us.

These horrors lead everyone at one time or another to the inevitable question: "If there is a God of Love, why does He allow all this cruelty?" We are here on Earth to learn a lesson. That lesson is that when humans break the Spiritual Laws of Love, suffering is inevitable. Once all humans have learned this lesson, and decide to follow God's Way, evil will be destroyed forever. God certainly does not want us to suffer forever. All humans will eventually love and appreciate God. That time will come.

What happens to the human spirit when we die?

When we die, the dust returns to the earth from which it came: and the spirit returns to God who gave it. The spirit of man has no life and has no consciousness without the body.

The analogy of a DVD video may help some understand this concept. The personality and the events of a person's life are recorded on the 'DVD', (the human spirit) but cannot be played back or viewed without a TV (the body).

When people die, they do not go to heaven, or exist in any other 'state', nor 'be' anywhere else, as the human spirit has no consciousness at all. In fact, no human being has ever ascended into heaven as the Word emphasises more than once.

God stores the human spirit of every human being until it is time for them to be resurrected. When the person is resurrected, God creates a new body for the person out of His Spirit Matter and re-creates the person by reuniting the new body with their spirit which contains all the information of their previous existence. How wonderful is that?

What about the resurrection we are promised?

If it is true that we 'go to heaven' when we die, what is the purpose of the promised resurrection?? That does not make any sense.

As Christ died on the Tree, He gave up the 'ghost' and His human spirit which had all His human experiences recorded on it returned to God the Father. He was stone dead, Then He was wrapped up and placed in a grave where He remained for three days and three nights. He did not go anywhere.

After His three days in the grave He was resurrected to human life and God placed His human spirit in Him. Christ Jesus then spent time with some people, and was seen by at least five hundred as proof of His resurrection but He did not allow them to touch Him until He ascended to the Father.

As He ascended to the Father in heaven, He was clothed with Immortality. He cleansed God's Temple with His blood, and His incredible sacrifice was accepted by God the Father to cover and redeem the sins of all human beings.

The now living risen Christ, Yahweh-Shua, then returned to Earth Immortal but in human form. He then showed himself to His disciples who finally recognised Him. Christ's resurrection was not 'done in a corner', it shook the whole world, and later thousands saw Him alive. The entire event is an irrefutable historical fact.

The 'Fall of Adam' was part of God's Plan

However, it was God's planned intention that Adam and Eve His very first children should eat of that tree so that they would have the knowledge of good and evil. Having this knowledge is an essential part of God's plans for all His children.

With the knowledge of evil and good, all human beings would be able to learn from their human experience that Satan's ways are the ways of death; and that God's Laws are the only true way to life and happiness.

Everyone on Earth would do well to recognise that God is indeed close to us, watching over each and every one of His embryonic family, and that God is not at all far away as some suggest. Our very existence is actually **in** God.

In a sense, the whole human race is in God's 'womb', the Earthly home within God's Invisible Heaven we have been born into. Nearly ten billion people are not really even remotely aware that they are alive and exist consciously as a gift from God, or that we are God's Offspring, or that a Father/child relationship exists between God and all humanity. How does that make God our Father feel do you think?

However, God has allowed all but a few humans to be blinded to Him by Satan so that God does not hold them fully accountable for their ignorance or arrogant defiance. According to God's Plan, this is not the time for most people to be given the gift of seeing the relationship humans can have with the Creator God. Most humans in their puffed up vanity do not appreciate that they are indeed 'tiny', and so very miniscule compared with the Great God their Father.

God has made everything intricately beautiful and He hath put the world in the heart and mind in such a way, so that no human can fathom the work that God created in every detail no matter how hard he or she tries. God keeps secret His knowledge, and in His Word, He exposes as nonsense the words of those who reject the 'Designer', and scholars whose 'science' has constantly to be updated and superseded by 'new' discoveries which prove that previous 'discoveries' were incorrect.

The Flood of Noah did happen

Adam and Eve had children, and their children had more children, and sadly they were all tarred with the same Satanic brush of giving in to the part of their own human nature that is enmity to God. Wickedness became epidemic, then pandemic, until God wearied of seeing the way His Children were behaving.

In 2369 B.C, or only 1656 years after man years after the Creation of Adam, God came to regret having created man, and changes His mind, and decides to destroy all humans, and the fauna, the animals that breathed on the Earth with the flood. God is not at all happy to strive with the human race and warns of the flood to come. That in one hundred and twenty years, God would destroy all but eight of them. Just one man had followed God's ways, and because of him, he and his family, eight in all, were miraculously saved in the Ark which Noah built under God's direction.

From these eight people, from Noah's three sons the whole Earth was overspread. Shem gave rise to the white people, Ham to the brown and black people, and Japheth was the father of all the oriental people on Earth today. Which shows how we came to have the different racial groups today.

So how is the story of the Flood relevant today? It is a warning for us today, in this era who indeed appear to be approaching the ends of the world to learn from. All the chaos in the world, serious climate change, unprecedented pollution of the Earth and its oceans, the renewed discussions of the further proliferation of nuclear weapons, the constant threat of the possibility of catastrophic nuclear war; all these factors certainly indicate that things are getting much worse, dire and not better.

Could we once again be headed for the almost complete annihilation of the human race? This time not initially as a result of God's intervention in human affairs, but now entirely due to reckless aberrant human behaviour. This is emphatically not 'fake news', 'media lies' or 'doom and gloom' talk, it is pure realism.

The 'birth' of universal rebellion against God
The human race increased in numbers over the next few hundred years, until it is thought to be around 2354 years after the birth of humankind, when humanity made another choice. Their activities and behaviour were universally against God's wishes. The Earth's population was not interested in living under an Invisible God they could not

see, they wanted a 'god' they could see, touch and feel. So at the instigation of Nimrod they built a tower to represent their 'god' which reached 'up to heaven'.

At that time, all the people of the Earth spoke the same language. God could see that this would only assist and empower the entire population of the time to speed up further rebellion against Him. So at the Tower of Babel, God divided tribes into nations and God also confused their language so that they could not understand each other. This was the origin of all foreign languages.

Up until the time of Babel, God had been working with humans, but this is when God is 'giving up' on the nations, and giving them what they wanted which was a 'god' of their own.

One word for 'God' in the Hebrew language is 'Elohim'. When the Word created spirit beings, some of them became the 'sons of God' who were 'lesser Elohim' but still a type of god rank. Very few people are even aware that such spirit beings exist. However they do, and they were and are part of God's Spirit Kingdom like angels who have responsibilities to care for and watch over humans.

In the early days, as human beings began to grow in numbers some of these spirit beings who were 'sons of God' could manifest, or 'morph' themselves into human form and have sexual relations with women. Some of the 'sons of God' lusted after the fair daughters of men and they chose them as wives who bore them children. In fact in doing so, clearly they had departed from God's service and become associated with Satan in his work of leading the people further away from God.

The children of these 'mixed' marriages were different from others. There were giants in the Earth in those days because when the 'sons of God' married the daughters of men, the children they bore to them became 'mighty men of renown'. Clearly the human children of the sons of God had considerably more powers than children born of humans.

These 'mighty men' were 'renowned' for what? They were powerful tyrants who oppressed the people, and lead their minds away from God. One such 'mighty man' was Nimrod who rose to great power and who set himself in opposition to God as a 'god' and commanded that he be worshipped by the people.

So many of the 'sons of God' defected to Satan's perverted way of thinking, and they became the unseen pantheon of gods that then ruled over the nations of the world and who still do so to this day. So God passed judgement on some of the 'sons of God', and told them because of their actions, they would die like men, but not all of them 'died'.

Some of the 'sons of God' had rebelled against God, and gone over to Satan's adversarial activities. Many of them were destroyed by God because of their rebellion, but others retained positions of authority under Satan to continue to influence human beings against God. Some 'sons of God' are very active in our era, some for good and some for evil.

Conspiracy theorists think that covert groups of powerful people hold sway over the events in this world. They undoubtedly do, but not in their own strength, they are supported by and influenced by the unseen fallen 'sons of God' who are doing Satan's bidding. Can some of them manifest or 'morph' themselves as human advisers of the 'Nimrods' of this present age? Are they the 'ones' inspiring the tyrants of this evil world? Perhaps.

It is likely that it was these 'sons of God' that became the 'gods' history records were worshipped by the nations through the centuries. The gods of Egypt, Isis, Osiris, Horus, Ra; the Canaanites, Ashtoreth, Baal, Chemosh; the Philistines, Dagon the fish god, a symbol of Dagon continues to this day with the 'fish' like hats of the church hierarchy; Greece, Zeus, Poseidon, Athena, Apollo; the Romans, Jupiter, Juno and Minerva. All these may well have been the actual 'sons of God' who could manifest themselves in human form, but also remain invisible as they held humans under their sway. Were the magicians of Egypt 'sons of God', or men working under their influence? Able to turn their staffs into snakes, produced a plague of frogs, and turned the river into blood? They clearly possessed superhuman or supernatural powers to be able to mimic the miracles performed by God through Moses.

Today our 'gods' have different names. The manner of human beings is to 'worship' almost anything they can think up, manufacture, or get involved with, even people as in the whole celebrity thing; any and everything except the worship of the true God and the result is ugly.

The history of the world's human beings ever since the Tower of Babel in 2354 A.M. or 1670 B.C. up until 4025 B.C. continued on its same path of rebellion against God.

CHRIST BECAME THE ONLY HUMAN BEGOTTEN SON OF THE FATHER

In 3 B.C., the time had come when God would move to save humankind from themselves. God loved his potential Family, and wanted them all to have the opportunity to 'live' and God was prepared to pay an awesome price to achieve His Plan. As planned aeons ago, the Word would relinquish his Power and position with the Father in Heaven and become a man.

God the Father had caused His Son to form the first Adam who was made of the Earth, Earthy, from the physical elements of the soil. The Father took the Spirit Matter of His Son the Word was made of and formed the human embryo which God placed into the womb of a woman. This human embryo would grow in Mary's womb, be born, and become Christ the Second Adam.

When the Word gave up His position with the Father, and became the human being Christ, Yah-Shua, the man born to the Virgin Mary, He became the first and only human ever to be the 'Begotten Son' of the Father.

It is an astonishing fact that among the billions of people who have some sort of connection or allegiance to the over 30,000 versions of 'Christianity' only a very 'few' understand the true origin of the Christ they worship. How many of them know and understand the true Nature of the Christ they worship? They speak of the 'sacrifice' of Christ their 'Saviour', but do they have any appreciation of just what that 'sacrifice' entailed?

The Word, the origin and true nature of who Christ was

The truth revealed in God's Word about the nature of God's Son who became our Saviour is astoundingly different from the world's view of Christ the Messiah.

The Universe, the Sun the Moon and the Planets of our system are all maintained and upheld continuously ever since His death and resurrection by the Power of the risen Christ, who Created it all in accordance with, and at the direction of the Father.

The awesome origin of Christ is amazing. He was the Word, the Creator of all things. The true heritage and nature of the risen and Glorified Christ who is currently upholding all things is not represented by the world of Churchianity.

Had all those religious people through history honoured God's commandment which forbids the making of graven images or the likeness of **any**thing in connection with the worship of God, the images, statues, stained glass windows displayed in so many churches would not exist; but they do.

Many churches have pictures that purport falsely to depict Christ. The figure, probably based on the god Zeus, is usually an apparently effete long-haired person in long robes. Such images should have never been thought of or even considered, let alone now to be a feature of so many places of worship.

Do they appreciate that their Lord Christ, was actually the Word, the Son of God who created the universe, the heavens and the Earth? That it is Christ Jesus who since His death and resurrection continuously upholds all things by the Word of His Power? Few churches, if any, preach this truth about God and His Plan.

The night before Christ was crucified by the Romans and stoned to death by the Jews, he prayed to His Father that He would restore Him to the Glory He once had with the Father. Christ knew about His origin.

As Christ suffered the unbelievably cruel double form of torture that resulted in His death, He became sin. His Father had to turn His back on Christ for that moment. Christ knew this, and cried out, "Why have you forsaken me?" The awesome penalty both the Father and the Son paid for the sin of humankind was profound beyond our understanding.

As Christ died, his human spirit returned to God. At the end of three days and three nights in the tomb, God the Father resurrected His only begotten Son Christ Jesus to physical human life. Jesus did not allow anyone to touch Him until after He had been carried up to Heaven, clothed with Immortality, had cleansed God's Temple in Heaven with His blood, and returned to Earth to show Himself to thousands of witnesses to His resurrection.

The testimony of those terrible events shows us that God and His Son so loved the humans of the world, which They were willing to go through that pain in order that their children would not perish, but would ultimately have eternal life as part of the Family of God. Human beings are destined to be heirs together with Christ our Elder Brother the heir of all things. Incredible.

God is now working through the second 'Adam'
There is an even deeper meaning by implication of the Hebrew word Yatsar used in the Bible when God was 'forming' Adam. It actually embraces the entire plan of God for His children. In 'forming' Adam physically so carefully from the red clay earth, moulding and shaping his whole body, and inserting human nature into his mind, God was also working with him spiritually. God much later in the story 'forms' the 'second' Adam, Christ who when resurrected and again with the Father now works with all humans 'forming' them spiritually through the power of God's Holy Spirit.

WHERE DO GOD AND HIS SON LIVE NOW IN THIS AGE?
God's Energy, in all its Forms, is Everywhere in the Universe. He stretches out the heavens as a curtain, and spreads them out as a tent to live in, and especially here near our Earthly home. God is not 'afar off'. He is right here with us, close to this Earth. God sits upon 'the circle of the Earth'.

God the Father and God the Son fill the Invisible Spiritual 'Heaven' which surrounds this Earth where the Father has His Throne and the Son sits with Him on the right hand of God, and the Earth is figuratively their 'footstool'.

Christ tells us not to 'swear by heaven; for it is God's throne, nor by the Earth; for it is his 'footstool'. What a lovely analogy.

They have their 'eyes' on every human being on Earth, watching over everything that is done here. The Power of God's Holy Spirit is Present everywhere. Especially with those who are 'the called'.

The Father and the only Begotten Son are One God. God now lives close by our Earth surrounded by His Invisible Heaven. In all the vast expanse of the still expanding universe, this is the area where God has chosen to live. This is where God will ultimately rule all that there is when "All is in All".

That Invisible 'Cloud' of God's Energy that surrounds our Earth is a type of 'womb' within which God is nurturing and nourishing His human children with both visible physical things and spiritual energies. So humans "should seek God, if perhaps they might feel they want to reach out for Him, and find Him, though He be not far from every one of us: For in God (in that cloud of Energy) we live, and move, and have our being; ...For we are also His offspring".

God in His Heaven is watching over His children continuously. The eyes of the Lord watch out all throughout the Earth for people who have given themselves completely to him whose hearts are completely committed to Him. He wants to strengthen them in their journey and He does.

CHAPTER 5

IS GOD REALLY GOD WORKING THROUGH 1000's OF DENOMINATIONS AND .ORGS?

There are supposedly more than 2.4 billion people who claim to be Christian in this world, but they belong to many thousands of competing churches, groups, and 'denominations'. Would the risen Christ, Yahweh-Shua, have a different way to deal with 1.285 billion Catholics, than with 920 million members of the Church of England, Lutherans, Methodists, Baptists and all the other Protestants? How about 270 million Eastern Orthodox, 86 million Oriental Orthodoxy, or 35 million in other 'isms' and 'dot orgs'? So if we think about that for a minute, how would Christ view these people? Is Christ 'divided' by all the dissenting factions in thirty thousand branches of 'Churchianity'? No.

So are all those 2.4 billion part of Christ's ecclesia, His group? Are some of them? We are not talking about whether people are sincere, well-meaning, or ardent in their version of 'Churchianity'. But simply to ask, are they really in touch with God, and are they following His wishes that He records in His Word the Holy Bible for us concerning the way they live their lives? Sadly in the vast majority of cases the answer is no.

A careful study of what 'churches' believe will reveal that there is not one 'ism' or .org which does not differ widely in their teachings from what God sets out in the Bible and requires of His human children. **All 'churches' wittingly or unwittingly engage every year in religious celebrations which God hates.** Most of those who attend churches have no idea at all that they embrace pagan, heathen traditions and practices in their special days of worship. People are either not aware, or think it does not matter, that the names of the days of the week and months we use every day are the names of false 'gods' that were worshipped historically. Ignorance is no excuse even in human law.

There are thousands of religious denominations in the world, many of which are riddled with idolatrous icons, have beliefs and attitudes, and **are involved in practices that God says He hates.** How has God dealt with people who choose to behave in ways that are directly against God's Laws and His Will? There have always been penalties for humans who rebel against their Creator, and there are today.

Do those who are deceived know it?

Anyone who is deceived, does not know they are deceived.

If they knew they were deceived they would not be deceived. Are you deceived about the religion, church or teachings you follow? How can you tell?

Here is a reality check for church attendees:

1. Are you comfortable to observe the Crucifixion and Resurrection of Christ over the 'Easter' period, when you understand that the word Easter comes from 'Ishtar' or Eastre, who was a sexually depraved murdering goddess of ancient Assyria. The Germanic Goddess **of** spring and dawn which was an ancient Sun worshipping and sex festival involving orgies, bunny rabbits and eggs held during the Spring Equinox? It is also the root of our English word 'estrogen' the name of the female sex hormone. How extraordinary that the root of this word has

continued over millennia, but its origins and meaning over time have been 'lost', and is unwittingly acceptable to religious people in their hundreds of millions. That period each year is a rather disgusting mixture of ideas is it not? Does it really matter? To God it does.

2. Is it appropriate for anyone to celebrate Christmas in December as Christ's birthday? No! Especially not when the *Winter Solstice period,* December $21^{st} - 25^{th}$, was observed as the 're-birth' of the Sun thousands of years before Christ. The Lamb of God was actually born on Nisan 1 on the Hebrew calendar in March/April time in the lambing season in Israel. Or is it right to perpetuate the incorrect charade of the 'Nativity' scene where Christ the baby is in the manger with the shepherds looking on, with 'three' wise men present (when actually hundreds of wise men had made the trek from the Iran/Iraq area) who did not actually meet Christ until two years later in a house?

3. How does God view 'All hallows e'en', Halloween with its Ghoulies, 'ghosties', Witches, and pumpkins with lights in to guide the 'spirits'? Often children demand treats with threat of tricks? Any activities which involve such things are so far from Christianity that they should be shunned and avoided.

4. Does it please God to see billions of people supposedly worshipping Him in churches full of images, statues, relics, all of which He explicitly forbids in His Word?

What have any of these practices to do with Christ or Christianity? Nothing! Are they Biblical? Absolutely not. <u>They are all abominations in God's sight. He hates all these activities, and tells us so in no uncertain terms in His Word. God wants us to avoid all these worldly practices.</u>

WHO and WHAT IS GOD?

God is extremely blunt in His language about the solemn feast days people have used to worship Him for thousands of years before Christ, and ever since. He calls them animal detritus or 'dung'. Like it or not, these are the Words of our Father God. (See Malachi 2:2-4) But most of Christendom has perpetuated these ancient celebrations to this day. When people attempt to worship God in ways that offend Him, in a sense they are putting their thumbs and fingers to their noses at Him like rude children are known to do.

Christendom practices a fatal mixture of truth and error which God finds obnoxious. Even the buildings they worship in are evidence of many pagan types of architecture which 'get up God's nose' like the phallic steeples, and the Sun 'worshipping' stained glass windows. So many churches built over several centuries were constructed on sites where Yew trees had grown for hundreds of years. Why might that have been so? Yew trees were worshipped by pagans and Druids because of their being evergreen and for their great longevity. When those churches were built, worshippers mixed in those pagan ideas with those of Christianity.

Churches and cathedrals are full of effigies and statues of 'saints', relics and other revered objects which some worshippers stroke and kiss. God says over and over again: Do **not** make likenesses, graven images, or any other thing connected with the wordship of Him. So that is just what people do.

The sheer numbers of ministers of religion who practice paedophilia and child abuse, as well as those who indulge in homosexual immorality is widespread among their ranks, and that shocking news has spread all around the world. The ministers of the high churches adorned in beautiful robes and skirts, or those with their collars on backwards, may look fine outwardly, but inwardly many are morally debased and spiritually bankrupt.

Christ says do not call anyone 'Rabbi', or 'Father' in a religious connection but millions do. Even the term 'Reverend' should not be used by clergy, as that is one of God's names. They are not to be revered, God is. If you think any of these statements are outrageous, perhaps some time spent in objective Biblical research might change your mind.

Nobody can serve or worship with any human organisation with their conflicting ideas of what God requires of His children **and** have a personal relationship with God the Father and Christ Jesus. No man can serve two masters, Christ is not divided.

Certainly, sincere people may think they are doing the right thing, but God thinks differently. People can be 100% sincere, but still be seriously wrong. Sincerity, even zealousness for beliefs that are a mixture of truth and error which people call 'Christianity' are actually an abomination to God according to His Word.

Beware of false Ministers, religions, churches
We have to be on our guard continually, as the subtleties of Satan guided people can appear to have attractive ideas and vain philosophies.

Seemingly religious people will often mention Christ and quote the Bible like Satan did to Christ when He was first tempting Him, but even the use of Scriptures can become a 'trap' for the unwary What these ministers or 'evangelists' say may seem to be very attractive, but only those who are alert to the subtle machinations of the Devil, and have God's Gift sound mindedness to recognise them for who and what they are can be safe. Yes, they may dress, look and sound in such a manner as to appear to be Godly, but inwardly they are as dangerous as rabid wolves. Christ warned about them.

And what are their 'fruits'? Oh, on the surface they may have all the appearance of 'holiness', but take careful note of the number of reports being produced daily about priests, clergy, and ministers being discovered to be involved in paedophilia, child abuse in all its forms, and other horrific immoral practices within their ranks. These reports and court cases are now a common occurrence as their victims finally come forward with the ghastly detailed evidence of their crimes, and the personal behaviour of clerics over decades is being revealed.

They are deceitful workers, passing themselves off as the ministers of Christ. And don't be surprised; for we are told that Satan transforms himself into an angel of light.

We need to avoid such people, and ask God to protect our minds from any such influences with the 'armour of God'.

So put on the whole 'armour' of God that you may be able to withstand the evil in the day, and having done this, to stand firm. Your loins girt about with the belt of truth, and having on the breastplate of righteousness; your feet shod with the gospel of peace; Above all, taking the shield of faith, with which you shall be able to quench all the fiery darts of the wicked. And take the helmet of salvation to protect your mind, and study daily the two edged sword of the Spirit, which is the Word of God:

The way 'to put on' this armour, is to be in touch with God and Christ daily through the daily practice of asking for Guidance, and spending time in the earnest study of God's Word the Holy Bible. It is imperative to avoid at all costs the religious ideas of deceptive men. Everything that happens to 'called' Christians is ultimately for their benefit.

Ten Essential Keys better to understand of the Bible

Key #1. First ask God for the help of Holy Spirit every time we study.

Key #2. God has written His Book in His Structure, Language & Styles

God's language is not our language. His way of thinking is not our way.

Key #3. Use a reliable translation, the King James is good but has errors. All translations contain errors, but don't let that put you off!

If ever in doubt about the meaning of any verse or passage. Check each word or phrase in the original manuscripts Hebrew, Greek or Aramaic using the appropriate resource.

Key #4. Be sure to check the context when studying any passage.

This key is very important to arrive at correct understanding of any Scripture.

Key #5 Check the grammatical syntax, and for interrogative adverbs

Look out for words like who, what, where, when, why, as these interrogative words sometimes reveal more much meaning when taken into account.

Key #6. Note the timing or chronology of the event.

Key #7 Take account of the geography where relevant.

Key #8 How to navigate the Scriptures, find words, verses, subjects etc.

There is an amazing, and incredibly fast way to find anything you are looking for in the Bible. People have done all the work of putting the entire words of the Bible in many versions and translations onto databases. This internet resource is free to use: https://www.biblegateway.com

Key #9 Set up a special working area, with all the necessary tools.

Pens, pencils, notebooks, a good reading light, comfortable chair.

Key #10 For your health's sake, get up and move around at regular intervals.

A five minute walk or other gentle exercise will rest and clear your mind.

So, who is God dealing with individually and personally now?
God has been aware of each of us and knew the potential of each of us personally long before the Universe was Created. Every human being who would ever live on this Earth was known to God individually long before the creation of Adam. Incredible, but true. God looked down the 'stream of time', and foreknew each one of His children before they were conceived. Talk about family planning!

Each person who has ever lived, or will live on this Earth, and today all nearly ten billion of them, are known intimately by God. Not only that, but God sees each one potentially as an adopted person in His Family. Amazing? Yes. It is the ultimate destiny of all people.

Does that mean then that everyone is in this privileged position from the moment they are born? No, it does not. Each person will come to this knowledge at the time when it is appropriate for them. God calls individuals to have a personal relationship with Him at His pleasure.

Many, if not all, have to go through a life of deception and alienation from God, until the moment when God decides to work with them personally. That moment when God decides to work with each of those who are 'the called' according to His purpose at that particular time.

The 'called, the 'few', have a fantastic calling, and it is not always an easy path to tread. But who ever said life would be easy?

Who is God working with specifically in this age?

God has always worked with individuals not organisations. Throughout history God worked with and through a selected few people, individuals like His Prophets, Apostles, and His human servants who He appoints over the nations. But what about this present moment, in our age. There is no doubt that God is taking a serious interest in the affairs of this world and His children.

Anyone who is thoroughly familiar with God's Word, the Holy Bible, will be aware that through the ages, God has worked mostly with individuals and families. In fact if one were to count all the people mentioned in the Bible as having been close to God and a part of His 'ecclesia' or group, they would be surprised at the relatively small number that God was directly involved with.

God is calling individuals at this time in history

Christ said that many are called but 'few' are chosen. God seems to be working with 'few' indeed in this era. Those who avoid church organisations and rely on direct contact with God for their inspiration are few indeed.

However, currently there are a 'few' who have God's special attention. They may or may not be connected to any organised religion. Those 'few' on Earth are the 'called' who have a special spiritual relationship with God.

These 'few' individuals do not concern themselves so much with the physical things of this life which are seen, but have in their minds and dwell on the things which are not seen. This is because the things which are seen are temporal (temporary, bound by time) and will eventually pass away; but the things which are not seen are eternal. (Age lasting, everlasting, for ever.) Many things in the unseen world are age-lasting and some are even Eternal. The 'called' have been given an opportunity to learn more about God and grow in Grace and Knowledge of His Plan.

The called 'few' now have the advantage of having direct contact with God and Christ by reason of being 'anointed' with the gift of God's powerful Spirit working in their minds. Notice, in that context Christ is telling us that we do not need any 'man' to teach us. God is working with each individual that He is calling and He gives each one only that measure of the Truth that is appropriate for that person at any given time. Also notice that 'the same anointing teaches you **of**', the word '**of**' here means 'that which is concerning and pertaining to some of'. It does not say it teaches you **all** things.

Each one of the 'called' receives their own measure of knowledge. Nobody can claim infallibility concerning **all** the truth, (especially this author.) but the 'few' can be sure that whatever God's Spirit teaches and inspires them to believe is the specific Truth for them at any given time. As we abide in Christ, we all have to grow in Grace and Knowledge. As we do, as His Spirit motivates us to express love, joy, peace, and so on, we are enabled to expand the action and effects of the fruits of the Spirit in the world around us. God creates that through us. How wonderful is that!

God knows each of the 'called' intimately, in every detail
Christ made it clear that God knows all about each of us, and if he chooses, even down to the number of hairs on our head. This may be literal or figurative, or both, take your choice, but either way, God knows all about us and cares about the most specific and individual aspects of our lives.

God gives us strength and protection
There is no real security on this Earth except the Love of God He has for His children that respect and fear to displease Him; those that hope in his mercy. He is our help and our shield.

They that wait upon the Lord, those that focus on their relationship with Him shall renew their strength; they shall mount up with wings as eagles; they shall run, and not be weary; and they shall walk, and not faint.

The 'called' of God are figuratively the 'apple of His eye', and have shelter under His 'wings' as chicks under a bird. He that lives in the secret invisible place of the most High shall be under the shadow of the Almighty. We will say of the Lord, He is my refuge and my fortress: my God; in Him will I trust. His truth shall be my shield. We shalt not be afraid for the terror by night; nor for the arrow that flies by day; Nor for the pestilence or diseases that walk in darkness; nor for the destruction that wastes at noonday. Even if a thousand fall at our side, and ten thousand at our right hand; but it shall not come near us.

God works with his 'ecclesia' His group - individually
Consider this. Every single person's DNA is different, everyone's fingerprint is different. Not only that, but no two

people on Earth are exactly alike in every way, or in every part of their lives, but God knows each of us in the minutest detail. He is our Father, and a Father who is totally Loving and Omniscient. He sees each of us, His beloved children, for who and what we are, and how we live our lives.

From His Heaven, the place where He lives, He looks on all the inhabitants of the Earth. He considers all their works. His eyes are in every place seeing both the evil and the good.

Human beings are not just billions of faceless people to our Father. He has a specific purpose in His mind for each of us. Hard to imagine, and almost impossible to believe, but this is what His Word teaches us. We need to ask for the gifts of His Belief and of His Faith in order for God's Plan to become a reality in our minds.

Ultimately human beings will be raised to God 'status' with Eternal Life as a Gift of God. Our role will be to live and reign with Christ, the King of Kings, in peace for the aeons to come. Reign over what? Over God's entire Kingdom the expansion of which has no end.

Even with all the technical advances, humans cannot really fathom the extent of the Universe. The vastness of it as it expands, the countless billions of galaxies and stars are all there to glorify God. His children are destined to be joint heirs, and to be a part of God's government of all this magnificent awe-inspiring array in the heavens, which is astounding.

Every human being will eventually be resurrected and then 'clothed' with a Sprit body, raised to God status, given Eternal Life, and inherit the Will of God. A more than incredible and amazing future awaits us.

Again, those human beings 'in Christ' at all times through history have been changed in nature to become a chosen race, a royal priesthood, a holy nation of people for God's own purpose to form Christ's ecclesia. This information is not widely known or appreciated by those among the organisations of Christendom.

The Christianity of 'Churchianity' has lost its way because of 'Attitude'

<u>Attitude</u> is the reason why 'Churchianity' is so very resistant to change,

When some people were asked "What do you think is the most important word in the English language?" Some said love, some said diligence, and others suggested acceptance, tolerance, patience, kindness, forgiveness, and other spiritual attributes.

The most important word and spiritual attribute is "ATTITUDE" This is because all other words suggested involve attributes which are determined by "ATTITUDE".

We pray daily, 'Thy Kingdom come.' And we need to have an objective attitude of continually 'watching' world events as Christ warned, while being fully aware of the true nature of the 'media' and 'fake' news. God will give us the wisdom to sort the wheat from the chaff.

Being set in our own concepts, ideas, and our ways is a fatal position, as is thinking we know it all. As far as Theology, Religion, Politics, Economics, Health, and for that matter concerning every topic under the sun, generally people are very resistant to anything new, and have a great reluctance to change.

The greatest fear for us humans is the fear of the unknown. Change involves the 'unknown' to a degree, and this touches the deepest fear humans have. All human beings have a great resistance to the fear of change. We all have this resistance built into our minds. This is nothing new.

WHO and WHAT IS GOD?

If we are to be mature people, serious Christians, and have a proper approach to life, we have constantly to be open to new information and be willing to make the necessary changes that are involved when we find anything 'new' is valid. We need to be in a continual 'attitude' of willingness to change.

Things we have believed in the past ten or fifteen years, a couple of years ago, even last week, or this very day, may need considerable revision, and we have to be constantly in an attitude of being mentally open minded. This too is a gift of God.

Resistance to change was very much in evidence in Christ's day. The Jews and Israelites wanted their own ideas to prevail, and had no intention of making any changes. Both the religious leaders and the attitudes of the populace were set like concrete in their 'tradition'. Over time, their oral law and Talmudic traditions had slowly become more important to them than the Mosaic Laws of God.

Interestingly, we see that the Laws of God were all in existence more than three thousand years before the Law of Moses was given to the twelve tribes of Israel. They were there in operation in the Garden of Eden with Adam and Eve, and with Noah in the Ark 1656 years later. Interestingly also, the food advice of God was clear to Noah, as God instructed him to take seven pairs of clean (edible, good to eat) animals into the Ark, but only a single pair of the animals that are not good to eat. The dietary laws in the Bible are not Israelite or 'Jewish' laws at all, but God's recommendations to humans for all time. They are good advice, but they are not <u>legally</u> binding on Christians today, but are still very useful to consider and act on.

Over hundreds of years attention to the 'Torah', the 'Law of Moses', the first five books (or Pentateuch) of the Holy

Scriptures, which contained the 'Mosaic Law' given to the Jews and Israelites by God Himself through His angel, gradually gave way to the 'Oral Law' of 'Traditions' invented by the religious leaders of the Jewish nation. Many of whom observe them to this day

The religious leaders were far more interested in laying down the law to people about the 'jot and tittle', the tiny matters of obedience to physical matters rather than the far more important matters of judgment, mercy, faith and so on. The religious leaders figuratively 'sit in Moses' seat which meant that they were those, who in the time of Christ, were responsible for explaining and maintaining God's Law, but they had changed their **attitude** to God's Law in favour of their traditions. Blasphemy? Yes.

Since the 'traditions' were not the Word of God, the traditions were far from perfect, they were onerous, tedious and invariably imposed emphases that were never intended under the Laws of God. The Pharisees had a rebellious attitude to God which indeed was opposite to the Love of God and His Law. They were proud exhibitionists, no meekness in sight. They wore phylacteries, little leather boxes attached to their skirts with parts of the Law embroidered on them for all to see, as some do in Israel to this day, but their hearts were not right. Are they now?

Whatever God says 'do not do', people 'do'. Jewish religious leaders of today who study and teach Jewish law are called 'Rabbi'. We know the largest Christian religious denomination in the world calls all their priests 'Father'.

Whatever God says 'do', they 'do not do'. This reveals the attitude and state of mind of those who claim to be people of God. It shows that they are in fact in rebellion against God. Pride of this sort, those who expect others to use titles when speaking to ministers, priests and so on, is not a Godly trait, but reveals in such religious leaders an attitude of self-aggrandisement, the exact opposite of the humility they ought to have.

The Jewish leaders of Christ's day were totally resistant to change, unless it involved changes they wanted to make in the application of God's Law, their 'traditions' were sacrosanct to them, and far more important in their eyes. It would appear that this attitude towards 'traditions' is just as rife today among the Jewish communities of the world, especially in the country of Israel where many of the Jewish men wear the 'Kippah', and still display phylacteries and 'payot' shaped beards, and long ringlets of hair at the side of their heads. Most Jews reject the whole idea that Christ was the Son of God.

We can often see pictures today of the 'Wailing Wall' (which was never part of the Temple) in Israel where the Jewish men clothed in black pray for hours, bobbing up and down for all to see. God instructs those who follow Him to pray in private, and we should follow that principle today.

Most of the religions of 'churchianity' do not understand the real nature of the 'Kingdom of Heaven' or the 'Kingdom of God', and when they insist on adherence to their false gospel, they prevent their flocks from truly understanding it either.

People who follow the dictates of 'Christian' religions of men have no idea that some of their beliefs, practices and behaviour are alien to the true Gospel of God. It is good for everyone to remember the truism:

A person who is deceived does not know that they are deceived.

When we pray, we ask for our 'daily bread'. This 'daily bread' does not only relate to physical food, but to spiritual nourishment as well. Christ is the 'bread of life' and the study of His Word is the means whereby we can obtain our spiritual food on a daily basis. We need also to pray to be delivered from evil or evil influences, and that He will protect our minds from deception.

Repentance means to change one's mind and behaviour.
Repentance is an old word. Since 1300 A.D., to repent has meant to feel such regret for sins or crimes mental or physical that it produces the desire to make changes in the way we live.

Repentance goes beyond feeling sorrow or regret. It involves the express and distinct intention for us to turn from 'sin', which is defined as breaking the law; to 'righteousness', which is keeping the law of Love. The words in the Bible most often translated 'repentance' mean a change of mental and spiritual attitude toward sin. A change of heart. We have to ask for that gift at least daily. Create in me a clean heart, O God; and renew a right spirit within me. Cast me not away from thy presence; and take not thy Holy Spirit from me.

It is essential for anyone claiming to be a Christian to be in a constant state of willingness to change, and a willingness to repent and change their minds and their ways, as God reveals new truth to them and as they grow in Grace and Knowledge.

Our *minds*, the way our brains think and reason, are our most precious possession. God holds us all responsible for the way we use our minds. We are exhorted to learn how to think like Christ thinks. Look not every man on his own things, but every man also on the things of others. Let this *mind* be in you, which was also in Christ Jesus:

We do not have to strive for Christ's mind, which is to keep our minds on God and the needs of others. It is ours as a free gift for the asking.

But as we have already seen, it is inherent in our nature to be resistant to change. While we might be emotionally 'in love' with God and His Gospel, AND we do have a fight on our hands. Christ says through Paul, "I delight in the law of God after the inward man: But I see another law in my members, warring against the law of my mind, and bringing me into captivity to the law of sin which is in my members", or indeed our whole being.

He went on to say that the good he wants to do, he does not do; and the bad he does not want to do, he does. I find then a law, that when I would do good, evil is present with me. Sad, but this is the experience of all who would be Christian, and we need constantly to ask for help to deal with our own nature.

We need to control our own human nature, not other people.
God's Word tells us in great detail how God wants His children to live. Although He can, God does not control His children. He wants each of them to be in control of their own lives, to choose of their own volition to worship Him and live according to His wishes. Self-control is a Godly quality.

The human desire to control others
Unfortunately, the desire to control others is part of our inbuilt human nature. The exercise of this desire is one of the root causes of all the strife in the world.

Whether between individuals, or where people are organised into groups, committees, churches, political parties or governments, the element of the control of others is always present. Listening to children at play ordering each other around are an absolute prime example. We learn to control others early in life.

Sadly, it is all too easy to be blind to our own glaring faults, while we pick at the minute failings of others. This is certainly something Christians will want to eliminate from their conduct with other people.

Once we are aware of them, we will observe that certain 'controlling' words are embedded in almost every conversation. It is so commonplace that unless we are cognisant and aware of the damage they can do to our relationships, we will not even notice them.

For instance, if the word 'you' is followed by 'should', 'ought', or 'must', this is a clear attempt to control the other person. It is not a good idea to tell others what to do.

There are other words best avoided. Like 'why' that calls the other into question, and puts them in a defensive stance. 'Yes but' which completely denies what the other person has just said. Telling people to 'try to' simply does not work; while anyone is 'trying to' they will never succeed. Popular 'soap operas' adored by millions are almost entirely built on characters that constantly blatantly attempt to control others.

Unless our work involves being 'in charge', or we are specifically being asked for our opinion, all controlling words are best left out of any conversation. Any comments that constitute orders, commands, warnings, threats, moralising, preaching, advising, offering solutions, suggestions, teaching, lecturing, logical argument, judging, criticising, blaming, name-calling, interpreting, diagnosing, analysing, probing, interrogating, or making adverse personal comments are all best not used at all.

To avoid controlling words takes a lot of attention moment by moment, and many years of practice to perfect. A powerful analogy might help. "As an arrow loosed from the bow, so a word, once spoken, cannot be recalled", no matter how much we might want to do so. The damage is done, and cannot be undone. Christians are urged to control the tongue, which is like the tiny rudder of a big ship. A tiny movement can have an enormous effect. The only 'control' we need to practice daily is self-control.

The spiritual armour of God protects us

We know that our human nature has components that are enmity to God. We need help moment by moment to stay in the Godly frame of mind. One help is to put on the whole spiritual 'armour' of God.

"Be strong in the Lord, and in the power of his might. Put on the whole armour of God that you may be able to stand against the wiles of the devil. For we wrestle not against flesh and blood, but against principalities, against powers, against the rulers of the darkness of this world, against spiritual wickedness in high places. So put on the whole armour of God so that you may be able to withstand in the evil day, and having done all, to stand".

We pray daily, 'Deliver us from evil' or the 'evil ones'. There is one part of the armour of God that protects the mind in our battle with our nature and the 'evil ones', the spiritual helmet. That 'helmet' protects the mind as we study and apply what we learn from the 'sword' of the Spirit, God's Holy Bible. Like all spiritual gifts from God, we have to pray to the Father and Christ and ask for that gift on a daily, and even moment by moment basis.

Love the Lord thy God with all thy heart, and with all thy soul, and with all thy **mind**, and with all thy strength and thy neighbour as thyself. This is the great commandment. Love God wholeheartedly, but the Golden Rule also includes loving everyone.

We are to put off, get rid of the conduct of our former person, which was corrupt according to the deceitful lusts built in to our nature; And be renewed in the spirit of our minds; And that we put on the 'new mind', which is created in righteousness and true holiness.

We have to take an active part in this renewal change, this repentant attitude, and work at it, always remembering that it is God who actually does the work. Here repeated for emphasis.

You do **not** have to "work out your own salvation with fear and trembling", so often quoted out of context. Because it is God which works in you, both to will and to do of his good pleasure. We do have to 'work' on ourselves, but it is actually God the Father and Christ who do all the work for us.

God leads us to repentance, and helps us change. Thank God.

These words: Mercies, kindness, humbleness, meekness (teachableness) longsuffering, patience, are burned into the consciousness of the fervent Christian and need to affect everything we think and do.

We are not given a mind of fear, but of Power and Love and a Sound Mind. We can rely on that wonderful gift of sound mindedness which we as Christians possess.

People who do not have the Spirit of God are not of a sound mind, just look at the state of the world today. People say that the world has gone mad, and they are right. The state of the world now is nothing like it was five, ten years, or a lifetime ago, it has so quickly slid down further into a morass, a mess of the worst types of sin. We should not smugly rely on the fact that we are on a Christian path, and relax, we need to be continually to be on our guard to be in a state of change.

We can see the dictionary meaning of *'repent'* involves *a change of mind, a change of attitude*. Repenting also means to possess the willingness to change continually in order to 'grow in grace and knowledge.

The first word Christ used as He began His Ministry was **'repent'**.

Certainly it is difficult even to address the need to change. Everything we do is habitual, it is hard to change any details. Breakfast, lunch, dinner, TV, are all routine events and we do not like them disturbed. Our journey to work usually takes the same route, with no exceptions, unless they are forced on us.

When Christ first began to teach, He got quite a warm reception from the Jewish Hierarchy and the public. As they witnessed the many healings, the miracles, some Pharisees and other religious leaders began to wonder if Christ was indeed the One to come. They thought He might even be the Messiah. As around that time so many were looking for that 'coming' of the King they were desperately hoping would sweep away the Roman rule.

Seeing all the miracles, others were moved, and wondered if this Man was perhaps the Messiah, and wanted to make Him the King that would save them from the oppressive Roman rulers.

But Christ was on a Mission from the Father to witness to all men. We can only imagine how the Priests, Pharisees, Jews must have reacted when Christ drove those who were trading in cattle and money changing out of the Temple, God's House. This would have upset the whole pattern of the accepted life in the Temple, and of course because there was a lot of money involved, this would have made those affected by Christ's actions very angry indeed.

But then the Jews posed another question to Christ, Yah-Shua. What sign will you show us, seeing that you do these things? He answered and said to them, Destroy this temple, and in three days I will raise it up. But the Priests and the Pharisees did not understand what Christ was talking about, their minds were only on the physical. But again the Jews asked Christ for a sign.

Then again certain of the Scribes and of the Pharisees asked for a sign from Him. But he answered and said unto them, "An evil and adulterous generation seeks after a sign; and there shall no sign be given to it, but the sign of the prophet Jonas: For as Jonas was three days and three nights in the whale's fishes' belly; so shall the Son of man be three days and three nights in the heart of the earth".

This sign they asked for was shortly to be demonstrated to them all. Christ's resurrection was not 'done in a corner', it shook the world, and more than five hundred saw Him after His three days in the grave and was resurrected. The event is a historical fact.

So, everyone began to get more out of step with Christ when He started to address the error of their own form of the Law, and show where they were wrong. They certainly did not want 'Moses' and **their** 'Law' to be changed by someone they considered as an 'upstart'.

If Christ would have gone along with the teachings, everything would have been fine, but He did not. They got more incensed until they stirred up the Jews, the crowd, and the Romans to get Christ killed, and of course, He was killed, stone dead from both the painful crucifixion imposed by the Romans, and the horrific stoning from the Jews.

The religious leaders of Christ's day were virtually committing the 'unpardonable sin', that of blasphemy against the Holy Spirit, as it seems are so many now on Earth, perhaps two or three billion people involved with 'churchianity' today. What a serious warning to us all to be very careful what we say in an 'idle moment'. Our daily communication is best just to be, 'Yes' or 'No, because whatever is more than these words can come from evil.

When a person changes from one belief to another, if that religion is part of the ruling state, and Christianity was at one time, the Roman Empire considered it to be treason. The Jewish leaders considered it to be blasphemous. So everyone rose up against Christ and chose to have Him beaten and slaughtered.

As Christians we need **to want to be** in a constant attitude of willingness to change, and it is always difficult to do so even with God's help.

As always, there are differences of opinion among those who earnestly seek God. Even among the disciples and Apostles, adapting to the new Truths which the risen Christ, YahwehShua was revealing to Paul presented a more than difficult challenge to them. There was the great issue about the 'Law' which those 'dyed in the wool' Jews, stuck in 'traditions', immersed in their view of Judaism, were not willing to it let go easily. What a wonderful relief it must have been though for those who accepted the 'new' truth to learn that physical circumcision was a thing of the past.

It is tragic that two thousand years later, some people think that they are superior Christians because they still attempt, and fail miserably, properly to keep aspects of the Law like the Sabbath and 'Clean and Unclean Meats', 'tithing' (which is actually illegal now according to God's Law.) and so on. They do not realise that by attempting to keep the Law (which is totally impossible), they are actually denying the life, teaching and sacrifice of the Lord who bought them.

The whole purpose of Christ coming to Earth was to free everyone up from bondage to the old law, and usher in His New Covenant of the Law of the Heart, and finally to reveal the 'mystery' to Paul in 64 A.D. It is impossible to keep one foot in the Old, and almost not even a toe in the New, and be a Christian, but blinded, they cannot see it.

Then when Paul learned about the 'mystery' in 64 A.D., he realised that both the Gentiles as well as the Israelites would be saved. They would be able figuratively to be 'in heaven with Christ' while alive. This absolutely infuriated James and Peter, and the Christians who still held on to the background of the Temple Laws. The 'mystery' teaching was so radical, it meant they had to make many more changes to the way they were used to thinking. Some even said that Paul had gone off his head, and was crazy.

Most around Paul had rejected the new truth that Christ had revealed to him. Everyone had abandoned Paul, and he was left to die a lonely man. It is no wonder God allows those who are in the 'ecclesia' now to feel they are all alone in this world apart from their close connection with Christ Jesus.

Some older people feel they cannot change. Abraham was seventy-five years old before God asked him to cross the river, and he obeyed. When he was ninety-nine, God gave him the ritual of circumcision, and Abraham had to make a HUGE change and follow God, which of course he did. An example of willingness to change at any age.

The result of these changes means that our relationship with God changes, and as we begin to learn more about Him and the way He thinks, we find we are able to love Him more than ever.

We have to be willing to change in this 21st century, or how can we grow in grace and knowledge? We all need to have the attitude of continual repentance, and it is beautiful and wonderful to embrace the changes that God sends to us in the development and expansion of His Government for His children.

__Attitude is everything. Willingness to change and continual repentance are the only safe way forward for those who are now 'in Christ'__

CHAPTER 6

THE NATURE AND HEART OF HUMAN BEINGS

According to God's Word the Bible, the carnal human heart is deceitful above all things, and desperately wicked: who can know it? Most don't, so humans start off at a considerable disadvantage when it comes to emulating the Love of God. However, God deals with each one of us individually He knows all our frailties and our strengths.

The heart 'attitude' in the Bible
Our first responsibility in the realm of love is to love God with all our heart mind and being. We need to realise that being saved is a gift, and know and appreciate that, regardless of anything we are or do, we are 'saved', and will one day be glorified and become part of the family of God. Absolutely no works on our part are needed, Christ did all the work that was needed for this to happen.

The word 'heart' in the Bible means the very inner being of a person, their mind, their feelings and their attitudes.

There are 884 words translated 'heart' in the Bible. They are used in contexts that describe many aspects of the human heart. If anyone wants to find the Biblical reference they could use the www.biblegateway.com site. It is free and very quick to use. Just put in the search box the word heart and press return. Then one can work through the books of the Bible and read any or all of them.

WHO and WHAT IS GOD?

Eternal life is a free gift for all, so what are Christian works?
Eternal Life is a Free Gift from God for all, it is important to understand that. There is nothing we have to do, or indeed can do to 'earn' salvation.

Although being 'saved' and being given Eternal Life freely, there is still a lot of 'work' for a Christian to do on ourselves if we are to earn some position of authority in the Kingdom of God and reign with Christ for a thousand years which is called the Millennium.

The internal 'work' we have to do on a daily basis is to control our human nature, and to bring our minds into submission to the Law of Love of God and our neighbour. As we have seen previously, we also have to control our desire to control others which is not a Godly trait. **Self-control is a Godly work. This can only be achieved with God's Spirit actively working through our minds. We <u>cannot</u> do it on our own.**

The external 'work' we are also required to do is the very best we can, in the use and development of the 'talents' that God gave us at birth, whatever they may be. Whether in design, or the arts, sciences, finance, agriculture, or the innate skill He gave us for anything in life, God wants us to make the best of those talents in service to Him and to other people. This is something else we need to pray about daily, that we will be 'worthy' to be in the Kingdom when Christ returns.

The spiritual treasures that each of us lay up for ourselves to be stored in 'heaven' will become a permanent part of us in our new life as fully fledged children of God. The more we use our God-given talents to develop Godliness, the greater will be our reward in the Kingdom of Heaven.

Two parables, stories with a moral, emphasise that in this life we are to be making the best use of our talents, our 'hearts' and our minds. The reward for our 'work' will be a part of our 'treasures in heaven'.

The Parable of the Talents or pounds

A 'man' (actually figuratively Christ) called his ten servants and gave them each a pound and told them to look after the money until he returned. Christ at the second coming, having established the kingdom, He then commanded these servants to whom he had given the money to be called to him (in the Kingdom.) so that He might know how much every man had gained by trading. The first, said, Lord, your pound has gained ten pounds. Christ said to him, Well done good servant: because thou have been faithful in a very little, have thou authority over ten cities. The second came, saying Lord, your pound has gained five pounds. And Christ said to him: Well done, you can rule over five cities.

The Parable of the Talents

The Kingdom of heaven is as a man travelling into a far country, who called his own servants, and gave them charge over his goods. To one he gave five talents, to another two, and to another one; to each man according to his personal ability; and straightway took his journey.

Notice, each one received according to their ability to handle money. Then he that had received the five talents went and traded with the same, and made them other five talents. Likewise, he that had received two, he also gained other two.

After a long time, the Lord of those servants came back, and called them to account. He that had received five talents came and brought other five talents, saying, Lord, you gave unto me five talents and look, I have gained beside them five talents more. His lord said unto him: Well done, you good and faithful servant: you have been faithful over a few things, I will make you ruler over many things: enter into the joy of your lord.

He also that had received two talents came and said, Lord, you gave me two talents: Look, I have gained two other talents beside them. His lord said to him, 'well done, good and faithful servant; you have been faithful over a few things, I will make you ruler over many things: enter into the joy of your Lord'.

Notice: Each of these parables or stories also tell of a person who did nothing with the pound or the talent he had been given to work with, so it was taken from them and given to those who had made the most of the talents they had. There is a powerful lesson there for everyone to heed. Although Eternal Life is a free gift, we need to use our God-given talents to the very best of our ability in order to merit an appropriate reward when Christ returns bringing His rewards for all with Him, and as He welcomes us into His Kingdom. Christ will bring His reward for us with Him when He returns. Each of us shall receive a reward according to their own work.

Those who would be 'greatest of all', in humility, will want to be servants of all in this life. To be a 'light', and to give help to all those in need where it is appropriate to do so. The state of billions in this world is precarious and parlous indeed, and we cannot help them all. We need to pray to God for wisdom about how to be selective in the way and the extent to which we can help others, and to pray for His Kingdom to come, and usher in His Government whenever that is to be.

Anyone who has neglected to do Christian works on the 'fruits of the Spirit', may miss out on a specific level of position, or may not even qualify to be in the initial Kingdom Phase. They will have to 'sleep' in death until the second resurrection at the end of the Millennium when all others who have ever lived, but not understood God's Ways, will be given an opportunity to be trained to become part of God's Family.

What does it mean to work out our own 'salvation'?
As we have already observed, we do **not** have to work out our own 'salvation' because it is a free gift from God. In this instance we are discussing here, it is not referring to what we know of as 'Salvation', i.e. being saved from death and given Eternal life. In this context covered here it is describing our part in the need consciously to allow God to 'work' in us, to deliver, rescue, or save us from our own human tendencies.

To grow in Grace and Knowledge we have to ask God daily, even minute by minute to cause His Holy Spirit to flow through our minds, our every thought, and our every action. We **canno**t do it in our own strength.

Work on living and acting out the 'fruits of the Spirit'
To embrace and develop in our lives each one of the fruits of the Spirit takes effort, labour and 'work'. The result of the nurturing the fruits of the Spirit does not come easily or naturally to us. The human mind has a wicked tendency which actually hates and fights the ways of God. We can see the types of wickedness that abound in this present evil world.

Some people give free reign to their lusts, which leads to all unrighteousness which is disobedience to God's Laws of Love; to deceit which fills the human heart, to anger, strife, maliciousness, hatred, murder, lasciviousness or indulging in an overt sexual interest, fornication or sex before marriage, wickedness, theft, envy, covetousness, endless debate, gossiping whisperers, backbiting and envy. To mention but a few traits so commonly 'accepted' by so many today.

The infamous 'seven deadly sins' are: Lust, to have an intense desire. Gluttony, excess in eating and drinking, obesity is epidemic. Greed, the problems of the whole world have their root in greed. Laziness, Wrath or strong vengeful anger. Envy the desire to possess other's things. Pride, inordinate and excessive self-esteem.

God's Word has His own list: There are six things the Lord hates, even seven that are detestable to him: haughty eyes, a lying tongue, hands that shed innocent blood, a heart that devises wicked schemes, feet that are quick to rush into evil, a false witness who pours out lies, and a person who stirs up strife among others.

That is quite a list of things for those who want to follow God's ways to avoid and to resist in themselves.

When under the stresses and strains of life, it takes real 'work' on our part to let God help us to allow ourselves to experience love, joy, peace, patience, gentleness, goodness, faith, long-suffering, meekness which is teachableness, and temperance or self-control.

We have to 'work' on our minds which always have the tendency at some level to resist God, and even be at enmity with Him, and war with His Spirit. It is only with the addition of God's Holy Spirit Power that we can even begin to do this very specialised 'work'.

We have to suppress our own carnal feelings like holding down a spring. A moment of inattention, and our minds spring back and revert to carnality. No human can do this 'work' effectively without the presence and flow of God's Holy Spirit in their hearts and minds.

The first and most important 'work' God requires of us is to fear to offend or deeply to respect the Lord thy God, to walk in all his ways, and to love him, and to serve the Lord thy God with all our heart and with all our soul (being), heart and mind.

God wants us to bear 'fruit' like a 'fruitful' tree planted by rivers of water. The 'fruit' we develop as we grow are spiritual 'fruit'. This requires us to be diligent in our 'work'. We need to ask God daily for more faith, and add to that faith He gives us we develop 'virtue' which embraces many qualities of character.

Virtue includes: Godliness, truthfulness, honesty, reliability, integrity, gratitude, temperance and self-control, patience, fairness, generosity, bravery, courage, joyfulness, respect, level headedness, charitableness, friendliness, brotherly kindness, warmth, humour, and more.

These are some of the qualities we need to be 'working' on daily, and developing with God's help. This will ensure that we will not be barren or unfruitful, but always growing in the knowledge of our Lord Jesus Christ.

But even 'sincere' people that lack these qualities, however religious, are blind, short-sighted and fail to see the need to develop them, and have lost sight that Christ expects them to pursue Christian works, will miss out on a reward.

The 'called' brethren who really do give diligence to these things will never fall short, and can look forward to being in the everlasting kingdom of our Lord and Saviour Jesus Christ at His coming.

The Human spirit, mind, 'heart', and attitude make up who we really are. While the human body is temporary, the spirit of a person is potentially eternal. This is why we are exhorted to have an attitude of constantly growing and developing our human spirit in Grace and Knowledge to become more like our Father and Christ.

WHO and WHAT IS GOD?

We need to develop the mind of Christ.

But what exactly is the mind of Christ? Everyone thinks about their own things, and that is good and right. However, everyone needs also to think and consider and be aware of the needs and things of others. While taking proper care of ourselves, our daily focus is to emulate the Love of God to the maximum of our ability.

God's love could be expressed as 'outgoing concern for others' as evidenced by His Love for us. Loving our 'neighbour' as ourselves. This is of course only one aspect of His love, but this should be our constant attitude of mind and heart every day.

We do not need to lay up treasures upon earth, where moth and rust corrupts everything, and where thieves break through and steal. Why not? Because everything physical about us is temporary, and will pass away when we turn to dust in death, or are resurrected into the Kingdom. Instead, we need to lay up for ourselves spiritual treasures of character development in heaven by doing Christian 'works', where neither moth nor rust corrupt, and where thieves do not break through nor steal.

Why does God want us to grow in Grace and Knowledge? It is because the attitude and practice of learning, development, and the training work on our human spirit and mind in the Word and Thoughts of God results in *permanent changes in our beingness.* God wants His children to grow and bear treasured 'fruit', just as human parents want their children to grow and develop in positive ways.

What happens when Christ returns?

When Christ Jesus arrives at His second coming, both those Godly people that are dead and those who are then alive 'in Christ' will be resurrected to life, and they will all rise to meet Christ in the air. This is called the 'first resurrection', although Christ was actually the First to be resurrected to Eternal Life.

These people who are resurrected will be all those since Adam who have answered God's 'calling' and have worked with Him on their talents during their lifetime. Those who are accounted worthy will at that time be given the opportunity to become part of God's Family. Those who rise to meet the Lord in the air, will be changed from human to Spirit in the twinkling of an eye and clothed with Eternal Life, and will rule with Christ in His Kingdom.

What happens in the 1000 year Millennium?

Those who have been 'saved' at Christ's second coming will reign with Christ for the 1000 year Millennium. They will learn in depth about God's Government and God's Law of Love, and also be trained as teachers to help those human beings who survived the Great Tribulation and live on into the Millennium to come to know God.

The 'saved' will teach those human beings who escaped death in the Great Tribulation about God and His ways, to repent of their past ways, and how to accept Christ and eventually become members of God's ruling Family.

Their 'teachers' will not be removed out of sight, but 'students' will see their teachers'. They will hear them instructing them day by day saying to them, "This is the 'way', walk in it, when you turn to the right, and when you turn to the left". Their teachers will always be around them showing them how to live and encouraging them in the 'Way'.

We have to be willing to change in this 21_{st} century, or how can we grow in grace and knowledge? We all have to have the attitude of continual repentance, and it is beautiful and wonderful to embrace the changes that God sends to us in the expansion of His Government.

Attitude is everything. Willingness to change and continual repentance are the only safe way forward for those who are now 'in Christ'

CHAPTER 7

THE DEVELOPMENT OF TRUE SPIRITUALITY

How does God go about promoting genuine spirituality, the love of God and for our fellow human beings? Most people think that God uses His Supernatural Powers in many ways to accomplish this. Yes, God does teach people how to both love Him and our neighbour which is everyone in the world. God can do this by both external and internal means.

In the Bible there is a good deal of evidence showing that God has applied many physical pressures on His children to further His purposes. But have those pressures He used in an external way resulted in permanent change in the attitude of His people, and enabled them to develop proper spirituality?

This use of external means to aid human development can be, and have been, beneficial in a temporary way historically, but very rarely if ever had a permanent or satisfying result.

What sort of external pressures has God used and will use in the future? They can be very profound. He has shown an abundance of miracles to people to demonstrate Who He Is. Like the miracles of the plagues of Egypt, parting of the Red Sea in the Exodus; or the daily provision of manna, tasty food in the desert for forty years every day except the Sabbath which was a miracle in itself. Also the fact that their shoes did not wear out as they tramped those forty years in the desert was a daily miracle for them to appreciate.

But did any of these miracles result in a change of heart in those Israelites, the people of God? No, it did not.

So apart from just two people, for their many rebellions against God during forty long years, all those nearly two million Israelites died in Sinai, and only their children were allowed to enter the Promised Land. One can read of an almost endless number of miracles where God has dealt with people in a physical manner but they have not resulted in a change of heart towards God.

Christ worked a huge number of miracles in the course of His ministry. They were evidence that Christ was a Special Person, and they affected many thousands of people. Some even believed He was the Son of God, others did not. Christ turned huge containers of water into wine, performed miraculous healings galore, fed thousands from a few loaves and fishes, and even raised the dead. These and many other miracles were certainly well known to the religious Pharisees and secular leaders. But the question is, did these miracles result in any significant change in the people of that time? No.

The entire population forgot all about the miracles He had performed and chose a robber to be set free, and crucified Christ. The effect of these awesome miracles on people did not last very long, did they?

And over the centuries since that time, has the knowledge of these miraculous events resulted in any permanent change in the spiritual attitude of humanity towards their heavenly Father? A quick view of history, and an objective look at the state of our present evil world, tells us that none of God's outpouring of miracles that show His Power and Love has changed the hearts and behaviour of humanity. Nor has it led them to become truly 'spiritual' according to God's wishes and intentions.

Miracles are one form of influence, but God has used many other means including external judgements and punishment for disobedience, even a religious system, the Mosaic Law, to control them, and these all run as a thread throughout the Bible. But have these punishments been effective or resulted in a permanent change of heart or inculcate spirituality in humanity? No.

What about when God put in force a religious system where people were governed from dawn to dusk every day of their lives and were forced to live in a certain way, and practice righteousness under threat of punishment, even death. Has that ever happened in history? It did under the Mosaic Law. Did it work to change people's minds and hearts in a permanent way? No.

Religious practices which people involve themselves in are all external. Although they may also have an internal effect, this does not always bring about any of the real form of true spirituality that God wants us to experience. The Bible shows very clearly that none of these three major pressures that God has used changed people. Neither did all the punishments result in any permanent change, nor did the miracles.

It is true that there have sometimes been some slight temporary benefits in some people, but punishment has not resulted in a permanent change in the way people behave or how they use their passions in sinful ways.

People may think of three things, miracles, punishment, and religion as the means whereby God creates spirituality, but clearly, they have failed to bring about any long-lasting development of proper spirituality. They have not had the effect of transforming the heart of humanity to behave in ways that are more like God's heart and character, with

His Love, His Wisdom, His understanding. Times without number in history shows that none of these things God has used have resulted in the permanent development of more Godlike behaviour in humanity.

There is only one 'Thing' that can bring about a permanent change, and that is the indwelling of the Holy Spirit in a person. God wants us to seek his gifts, the important ones are the spiritual gifts of love, compassion, belief, repentance, joy and so on.

Miracles galore are coming in the near future. A man, a false prophet calling himself 'God' and his associate the Beast will sit in a newly built temple, and will perform more and greater miracles than seen in the whole of history. What will the result be? One day we will know.

God will also send two witnesses so that the True Gospel is preached throughout the world, but the 'world' kills them, and then people will send presents to each other to celebrate.

God will then shower the Earth with miraculous horrendous devastating plagues, but this still does not cause the people to repent. The rebellion of the population of the whole world against God will be the result.

People do not learn from miracles.

There is only one thing that is going to bring in true spirituality, and that is LOVE. Love for God, Love for neighbour, and for all humanity and for everything that is in the universe, and that is very difficult for us to do. The first thing we need is to realise that even to start on this pathway to spirituality, we have to ask God for the gift of Holy Spirit, and the attendant gifts of belief, faith, and repentance. Whosoever drinks of the 'water' of the Holy Spirit that I shall give him shall never thirst; but the water that I shall give him shall be in him a well of water springing up into everlasting life.

God wants to Love us, and He shows this to us in so many ways. If sometimes trials and even what might seem like punishments come our way, provided we take them as God loving us, then we will have developed, with His help, a degree of true spirituality.

Love is the Key to everything. To love God with all your heart mind and soul, and your neighbour as yourself is the answer to all the problems of being human. Love never fails. We also have to love and respect ourselves, as we can only love and respect others to the extent that we love ourselves.

Honour your father and your mother: and, you shall love our neighbour as yourself. That is the Golden Rule. We could pray: **I will not treat others the way <u>I think</u> they ought to be treated; I will ask God to help me to treat others the way <u>they would like to be treated.</u>**

Christ gave up his position with the Father, to be a man, who bore the sicknesses of the world, and was totally degraded and humiliated. This is what humans did to Christ. It shows that He was willing not only to become a human to suffer this terrible fate, but how God the Father showed His immeasurable love for us.

Despite all Christ did for us, does that really help us to bear the sufferings of this life? He completely understands what it is like to be human. It should and does help us through this life, and it does more so when we are diligent in our contact with Him.

But what leads us to the best form of spirituality. God Almighty shows you literally that he loves YOU, yes you reading this. The disciples began to argue about who should hold which position. So Christ began to serve the meal and then washed the disciple's feet. The Creator of all things showed by example how He loves us by His serving His disciples. He shows us the Way that whoever would be the greatest of all, will be willing to be servant of all. That is true Spirituality.

The Glorious future of Human Beings
One day, when the Kingdom of God is established on this earth, and God's human children are introduced to the reality of Christ and His Power, they will have a huge awakening to the reality of God and His Plan for us which is quite beyond our ability to comprehend at this time.

The Word was appointed to be heir of all things, and as His children, human beings will also become heirs of all things in the Family of God.

Satan has deceived the whole world – why does God allow it?
When God says that Satan has deceived the whole world, He means just that. Of the nearly ten billion people on earth, how many of them are deceived? Nobody can say, but clearly the vast majority of them do appear to be.

When we look at the world in an objective way, we see that so much of what humans are doing under Satan's sway is chaotic and destructive.

So many people ask, "If there is a God of Love, why does He allow all the terrible suffering in the world?" It is certainly hard to understand and accept that a God of Love would allow the horrendous scale of cruelty, and of the inhumanity of humans to each other. However there is a very good reason for it.

Pain and suffering are the result of human beings giving in to, and giving free reign to the worst side of human nature. It is an essential part of the Plan of God to educate His children and to teach them the awful consequences of breaking His Laws of Love. Human beings have to learn the difference between good and evil now, because God cannot and will not have disobedience to His Laws in the Glorious Kingdom that He intends us to inherit.

Even if a person is given this explanation, it is still hard for many to accept it. There is a way forward. 'Faith' and 'Belief' are needed. They are Spiritual gifts that God gives to those who ask for it. It is still a quandary for many. Without faith and belief in a God of Love, they are unlikely to ask for these gifts. Without them, they find it difficult if not impossible to understand the reason for the apparent contradiction of a God of Love, and the deadly natural disasters, the painful diseases, all the hate filled human activities, and the ghastly result of the wars of this world.

Humanity is wrecking our Planet
It is now becoming clear that we are wrecking the balance of the natural order of our planet at a disastrous rate.

Climate change, argued about over decades, is clearly now a reality. Now in 2019, scientists think that the stability of the entire world's eco system is at risk of fatal collapse within ten years. The consequence of the rise in the temperature of just 1°C in the oceans is giving rise to ever more violent storms, tornados, hurricanes and tropical cyclones. Arguments still rage as to whether this is due to the burning of trillions of tons of fossil fuels extracted from the Earth, the destruction of rain forests, unnatural agricultural practices, or whether it would have just 'happened' anyway. Those who understand that the Earth was formed to be inhabited know that the polluted air, the current appalling weather, the thousands of species we are now making extinct was not intended.

A large part of the Bible contains descriptions of future events which are known as prophecies. It is matter of record that those concerning past events have all come to pass. There are also warnings of future events to occur at the 'end of the age' which we need to be aware of.

Some Bible prophecies concerning the future ahead of us now read like a modern day newscast. Christ Jesus warns of Wars, famines, natural disasters, corrupt governments, disease epidemics due to poor hygiene and bad diets are pandemic, and will cause global cataclysmic destruction .

WARS

World War 1 in which up to 40 million people died was famously said to be "The War to end all wars". It was not. WW1 was followed only twenty years later by WW2 during which 60 million people died.

There has been a continuous stream of wars ever since the end of WW2. The total number of deaths caused by war during the 20th Century has been estimated at 187 million and is probably higher. All over the world many dreadful wars continue now in the 21st century.

Human beings do not learn from history.

The 'Great Tribulation'

The following information is not included in this book to frighten or worry people. If someone sees a person about to step in to the road in front of a speeding truck, they would want instantly to warn them before they took the fatal step. Those who understand the certainty of prophecy, and know without doubt that they will be fulfilled when it is time, are obliged to warn those who will listen. And forewarned is forearmed.

Christ Jesus warned of a period some time ahead of us, probably about three and a half years in duration, which would be a time of trouble, of 'great tribulation', a period of far worse hideous worldwide destruction than anything since the beginning of the world to that time, and never will be again. It will be so bad that unless those days should be shortened by God's intervention no flesh would survive it, but thankfully for the 'elect's' sake those days shall be shortened.

The destruction of 'all flesh' by human activity was not possible until the invention of nuclear weapons. So this prophecy written over two thousand years ago was definitely for a future time. It is not known how many horrific nuclear explosions it would take to erase the life of all people and animals.

Some estimate it would only take a thousand or so to pollute the Earth with so much radiation that nothing would survive. Nine countries together already possess around 15,000 nuclear weapons. The United States and Russia maintain roughly 1,800 of their nuclear weapons on high-alert status ready to be launched within minutes of a warning.

Now in very recent times in the 21st century, we need to face 'head on' the insanity of some world leaders. Is 'insanity' too strong a word? A few men at the head of the most powerful countries in the world are seriously discussing the further development and the production of yet **more** nuclear weapons. Is that not an insane prospect?

The majority of people in the world ignore God's laws and worship human 'idols' and the false 'gods' of self, money, sex, food and gluttony, pseudo-science, religion, drugs, beauty, education. Even those involved in Churchianity and its deadly mix of truth and error who think they are worshipping the true God are definitely not. Far from it.

The Bible tells us that before Christ returns, two men called the 'Beast' and the 'False Prophet' will sit in the new Temple that will be built in Jerusalem. That 'man of sin' will be revealed, the son of perdition, who opposes and exalts himself above all that is called God, or that is worshipped; so that he as 'God' will sit in the temple of God, claiming that he is God. And the whole world will believe him.

This man will actually claim to be Christ returned to Earth and the whole world will be fooled by him, and believe that he really is Christ. God will send the population of the earth a strong delusion so that they will believe this lie. Only those who have God's Holy Spirit will be able to resist this lie, and be protected as Christ arrives.

This false Christ will have warned the whole world by the media that Earth is about to be invaded by 'aliens' who are coming to destroy us and the nations of the Earth will have mobilised their armies and put them on a war alert.

This is very significant because when the true Christ Jesus does return with all His saints and they are encircling the earth for every eye to see, He and His saints will shower plagues on all who fight Him. Then the world's armies will turn to fight Christ as He arrives, and He will be forced to conquer them.

And Christ will fight against those nations who have assembled their forces to fight Him at His coming. Their flesh will supernaturally consume away where they stand, and their eyes will consume away in their sockets, and their tongues shall consume away in their mouth, so people will be convinced that 'aliens' are attacking them.

But finally, after some time when the fighting is all over, Christ's feet will stand on the mount of Olives, which is before Jerusalem on the east, and the mount of Olives shall cleave in the midst thereof toward the east and toward the west, and there shall be a very great valley; and half of the mountain shall remove toward the north, and half of it toward the south.

And the Lord will establish His Kingdom and be king over all the earth: in that day shall there be one Lord, and his name one. And He will reign over the whole world with His saints.

Our Salvation - planned before the world began.
He has chosen us 'in him' before the foundation of the world, that we should be holy and without blame before him in love. The 'called' who are now 'in' Christ were known to God and His Son before the Creation of all things. The 'called' are now in a very special relationship with God and Christ.

They are referred to as a chosen generation, a royal priesthood, an holy nation, a peculiar people; that should show forth the praises of Him who has **called them out of darkness** into his marvellous *light*; And in a figurative sense, those who are alive and 'in Christ' are now, at this time, *figuratively* with Christ in Heaven who is sitting at the Right Hand of God.

Who are the 'Called'?
Many are called, but few are chosen. The chosen 'few' are rarely people of great position or status in this life, but are those who God wishes to work with who have a contrite heart, and are willing to have a deep respect for His Word.

Notice not many 'wise after the flesh' are called, who in truth make themselves fools by denying their Creator. The word 'meek' means teachable, and it is usually those who have that character trait that God calls and uses to build his ecclesia.

God says, these are the people I am pleased with and upon whom I look: those who are not proud or stubborn but are humble and contrite in spirit and who respectfully fear my word.

The seemingly very 'few' that are the 'called' have access to God's Holy Spirit flowing through their hearts and minds in feelings, thoughts, inspirations, concepts, and ideas. Because of this 'few', or the 'called', have a very special relationship with God and His Son Christ Jesus. For in the same way as we hu-mans are 'in' God, when 'called' indeed are having their eyes and ears opened at this time.

When Christ said that He would build His 'ecclesia', his group, His body, He meant just that. He did not mean that He would allow any human organisation of any kind to be involved. Christ was not going to build His 'ecclesia' on Peter the pebble (petros), but upon this Rock (petra), Christ Himself would build His group.

Anyone who is a true Christian knows only too well how lonely a pathway the Christian life can be. It is very difficult to find another Spirit lead Christian to associate with. But those who are led by God's Holy Spirit in their minds know that God's Spirit does indeed witness with our human spirit.

When a person is given the gift of God's Holy Spirit in their minds God inspires them, breathes into that person, knowledge and understanding of His truths. They also receive other Spiritual gifts of belief, repentance, and the earnest desire to live up to the letter and the Spirit of the New Law that Christ brought.

When a person has God's Spirit, it illuminates the mind and heart of that person via the spirit in man given to them with their first breath. It gives each person the gift of the ability to 'see' themselves, and of their need to change.

The Joys of the Called, their freedom in Christ

But the 'called' have an absolute assurance that nothing can separate them from God's Love. Christians who follow Christ are called to come out of the 'darkness' of this world, and into the 'light' of Christ, because you are indeed a chosen generation, a royal priesthood, a holy nation, a special people; so that you can show forth the praises of Him who has called you out of darkness into His marvellous light; Again repeated for emphasis as this is such an incredible statement from our Saviour that we can absolutely rely on.

Christ said to His disciples in private, and to all those who are Christian disciples today that you are the **light** of the world. Let your **light** so shine before men, that they may see your good works, and glorify your Father which is in heaven. Those who are the 'called', who are led by Christ with His Spirit, have the light of life, a special form of **'light'** that enables them clearly to see the 'darkness' of this evil world.

Many have observed that 'lights' do not make any sound, unless they are malfunctioning. It is not what we say that counts, but what we do. We are saved by Grace as a Gift through Christ's works; and our 'light' is to be our 'good works' which we are commanded to perform, but even those 'works' we perform as Christians are the work of God in us and not from or by our own strength.

Our Glorious Hope of the resurrection and Eternal Life
In the Bible, the 15th chapter of the book of 1st Corinthians is called 'the resurrection' chapter. Here it is in a translation, which although not entirely in modern English or easy to read, but does give the exciting details about the future of Eternal Life for believers.

1 Corinthians 15:1 Moreover, brethren, I declare unto you the gospel which I preached unto you, which also you have received, and wherein you stand; 2 By which also you are saved, if you keep in memory what I preached unto you, unless you have believed in vain.

3 For I delivered unto you first of all that which I also received, how that Christ died for our sins according to the scriptures; 4 And that he was buried, and that he rose again the third day according to the scriptures: 5 And that he was seen of Cephas (Peter), then of the twelve: 6 After that, he was seen of over five hundred brethren at once; of whom the greater part remain alive to the present, but some have died.

7 After that, He was seen of James; then of all the apostles. 8 And last of all He was seen of me also, as of one born out of due time. 9 For I am the least of the apostles, that am not meet (fit) to be called an apostle, because I persecuted the assembly of God. 10 But by the grace of God I am what I am: and his grace which was bestowed upon me was not in vain; but I laboured more abundantly than they all: yet not I, but the grace of God which was with me. 11 Therefore whether it were I or they, so we preach, and so you believed.

12 Now if Christ be preached that he rose from the dead, how say some among you that there is no resurrection of the dead? 13 But if there be no resurrection of the dead, then is Christ not risen: 14 And if Christ be not risen, then is our preaching vain, and your faith is also vain. 15 Yes, and we are found false witnesses of God; because we have testified of

God that he raised up Christ: whom he raised not up, if so be that the dead rise not. 16 For if the dead rise not, then is not Christ raised: 17 And if Christ be not raised, your faith is vain; ye are yet in your sins. 18 Then they also which were dead in Christ are perished.

19 If in this life only we have hope in Christ, we are of all men most miserable. 20 But now is Christ risen from the dead, and become the 'firstfruits' of them that died. 21 For since by man came death, by man came also the resurrection of the dead. 22 For as in Adam all die, even so in Christ shall all be made alive. 23 But every man in his own order: Christ the firstfruits; afterward they that are Christ's at his coming.

24 Then cometh the end, when He shall have delivered up the kingdom to God, even the Father; when he shall have put down all rule and all authority and power. 25 For he must reign, till he hath put all enemies under his feet. 26 The last enemy that shall be destroyed is death.

27 For he has put all things under his feet. But when he says all things are put under him, it is manifest that he is excepted, which did put all things under him. 28 And when all things shall be subdued unto him, then shall the Son also himself be subject unto him that put all things under him, that God may be all in all.

35 But some man will say, How are the dead raised up? And with what body do they come? 36 You fool, that which you sow does not grow unless it dies: 37 And that seed which thou sow, you do not sow the plant that shall be, but it bares grain, it may chance be of wheat, or of some other grain: 38 But God gives it a shape as it has pleased him, and to every seed produces its own plant.

39 All flesh is not the same flesh: but there is one kind of flesh of men, another flesh of beasts, another of fishes, and another of birds. 40 There are also celestial bodies, and bodies terrestrial: but the glory of the celestial is one, and the glory of the terrestrial is another. 41 There is one glory of the Sun, and another glory of the Moon, and another glory of the stars: for one star differs from another star in glory.

42 So also is the resurrection of the dead. The physical body is sown in corruption; it is raised in incorruption: 43 It is sown in dishonour; it is raised in glory: it is sown in weakness; it is raised in power: 44 It is sown a natural body; it is raised a spiritual body. There is a natural body, and there is a spiritual body.

45 And so it is written, the first man Adam was made a living soul; the last Adam was made a quickening spirit. 46 Howbeit that was not first which is spiritual, but that which is natural; and afterward that which is spiritual. 47 The first man is of the earth, earthy; the second man is Christ the Lord from heaven.

48 As is the earthy, such are they also that are earthy: and as is the heavenly, such are they also that are heavenly. 49 And as we have borne the image of the earthy, we shall also bear the image of the heavenly.

50 Now this I say, brethren, that flesh and blood cannot inherit the kingdom of God; neither doth corruption inherit incorruption. 51 Behold, I shew you a mystery; we shall not all die, but we shall all be changed, 52 In a moment, in the

twinkling of an eye, at the last trump: for the trumpet shall sound, and the dead shall be raised incorruptible, and we shall be changed.

53 *For this corruptible must put on incorruption, and this mortal must put on immortality.* 54 *So when this corruptible shall have put on incorruption, and this mortal shall have put on immortality, then shall be brought to pass the saying that is written, Death is swallowed up in victory.*

55 *O death, where is thy sting? O grave, where is thy victory?*
56 *The sting of death is sin; and the strength of sin is the law.*
57 *But thanks be to God, which giveth us the victory through our Lord Jesus Christ.*

58 *Therefore, my beloved brethren, be steadfast, unmoveable, always abounding in the work of the Lord, forasmuch as ye know that your labour is not in vain in the Lord.*

People who are alive or dead in Christ will be changed at Christ's return

The 4th chapter of the book of 1st Thessalonians tells us:

13 *But I would not have you to be ignorant, brethren, concerning them which are dead, that you sorrow not, even as others which have no hope.* 14 *For if we believe that Jesus died and rose again, even so them also which are dead in Jesus will God bring with him.* 15 *For this we say unto you by the word of the Lord, that we which are alive and remain unto the coming of the Lord shall not precede them which are dead.*

16 *For the Lord himself shall descend from heaven with a shout, with the voice of the archangel, and with the trump of God: and the dead in Christ shall rise first:* 17 *Then we which are alive and remain shall be caught up together with them in the clouds, to meet the Lord in the air: and so shall we*

ever be with the Lord. 18 So comfort one another with these words.

The Revelation of the Future, the coming of the New Heaven and Earth

Then, in the last book in the Bible, Revelation that God the Father wrote, and Christ gave to John via an Angel in nearly 100 A.D., we learn of the 'end of the world' as we know it.

The Book of Revelation is not at all easy to understand. It is full of imagery, and a mixture of analogy, factual and figurative language. But it is awe inspiring, and we certainly benefit from being aware of what it is telling us about the future ahead of us. Even if we do not understand it all, it gives us a mental 'picture' of prophesied events to occur sometime in the future.

It is suggested that anyone reading this looks at chapters 20, 21 and 22. If a person is not familiar with the English of the 500's A.D., in the King James Version, it might be best to use a modern translation which is easier to understand

The almost unbelievable fact that all human beings are God's children, and that we are to inherit eternal life in the Kingdom of God when Christ Jesus returns, or at a future resurrection, is not an easy concept to grasp, credit or believe.

What a privilege to be one of the 'called' in this life at this time.

What an amazingly wonderful glorious future we have in prospect. Praise God, Hallelujah.

God speed Christ's Second Coming and the Establishment of the Kingdom of Heaven. Thy Will be done in Earth as it is in Heaven. Amen.

Postscript

Postscript: Let the words of my mouth, and the meditation of my heart, and my writings be acceptable in thy sight, O Lord my strength, and my redeemer.

BHB September 2023

www.ingramcontent.com/pod-product-compliance
Lightning Source LLC
Chambersburg PA
CBHW050435010526
44118CB00013B/1531